Troubleshooting iOS

Solving iPhone and iPad Problems

Paul McFedries

Apress®

Troubleshooting iOS

Paul McFedries
Toronto, Ontario, Canada

ISBN-13 (pbk): 978-1-4842-2444-1   ISBN-13 (electronic): 978-1-4842-2445-8
DOI 10.1007/978-1-4842-2445-8

Library of Congress Control Number: 2016962197

Managing Director: Welmoed Spahr
Lead Editor: Aaron Black
Technical Reviewer: Marty Minner
Editorial Board: Steve Anglin, Pramila Balan, Laura Berendson, Aaron Black, Louise Corrigan, Jonathan Gennick, Robert Hutchinson, Celestin Suresh John, Nikhil Karkal, James Markham, Susan McDermott, Matthew Moodie, Natalie Pao, Gwenan Spearing
Coordinating Editor: Jessica Vakili
Copy Editor: Karen Jameson
Compositor: SPi Global
Indexer: SPi Global
Artist: SPi Global

Distributed to the book trade worldwide by Springer Science+Business Media New York, 233 Spring Street, 6th Floor, New York, NY 10013. Phone 1-800-SPRINGER, fax (201) 348-4505, e-mail orders-ny@springer-sbm.com, or visit www.springeronline.com. Apress Media, LLC is a California LLC and the sole member (owner) is Springer Science + Business Media Finance Inc (SSBM Finance Inc). SSBM Finance Inc is a **Delaware** corporation.

For information on translations, please e-mail rights@apress.com, or visit www.apress.com.

Apress and friends of ED books may be purchased in bulk for academic, corporate, or promotional use. eBook versions and licenses are also available for most titles. For more information, reference our Special Bulk Sales–eBook Licensing web page at www.apress.com/bulk-sales.

Any source code or other supplementary materials referenced by the author in this text are available to readers at www.apress.com. For detailed information about how to locate your book's source code, go to www.apress.com/source-code/. Readers can also access source code at SpringerLink in the Supplementary Material section for each chapter.

Printed on acid-free paper

Contents at a Glance

Contents

About the Author

Paul McFedries is an iOS expert and full-time technical writer. Paul has been authoring computer books since 1991 and has more than 90 books to his credit, which combined have sold more than four million copies worldwide. Paul is also the proprietor of Word Spy (http://www.wordspy.com), a website devoted to lexpionage, the sleuthing of new words and phrases that have entered the English language. Please drop by Paul's personal website at http://www.mcfedries.com or follow Paul on Twitter at twitter.com/paulmcf and twitter.com/wordspy.

Introduction

More than ever, tens of millions of people rely on iOS to perform many of their daily tasks. These include not only typical mobile phone tasks such as calling and texting, but also smartphone/tablet tasks such as surfing the Web, sending and receiving email, taking photos and videos, getting directions, scheduling appointments, and using apps. Our iOS devices also contain crucial information that we need to access regularly, including our contacts, bookmarks, notes, and calendars. Increasingly, each of us sees our device as an extension of our self, making this the most crucial tool in our day-to-day lives and, so, the one indispensable device.

So it is no wonder that our lives are upset, possibly even derailed temporarily, when our iOS device doesn't work the way it should (or the way we think it should). If an email doesn't go through, web page text is difficult to read, or an app freezes, our productivity (and possibly our sanity) suffers. In such situations, all we want is for things to return to normal so our lives can get back on track.

But how do we get our iOS device to act normally again? After all, the iPhone and the iPad are the devices that are supposed to "just work." Glitches and hiccups and crashes just aren't supposed to happen with iOS. Alas, they happen all too often and most of the time it isn't obvious not only why the problem occurred, but what can be done to fix it (and prevent it from happening again in the future).

Welcome

Welcome, therefore, to *Troubleshooting iOS*. In this book, you learn how to prevent iOS problems from occurring and (just in case your preventative measures are for naught) how to fix many common problems yourself. It is those nonobvious fixes, workarounds, and preventative measures that form the core of this book. In clear, straightforward, easy-to-understand prose, this book takes you through dozens of iOS problems, in each case giving you both some background about why the problem occurred and one or more ways to solve the problem and get the device (and *you*) back in business.

Who Should Read This Book?

When an iOS problem occurs, there are a number of troubleshooting resources available. These include contacting Apple Support, searching Apple discussion forums, taking the device to the Genius Bar, or self-diagnosing the problem. You should read this book if you're an iOS user who has some experience with the device, but who, due to a lack of time, interest, or inclination, isn't willing or able to perform these standard troubleshooting steps. For people like you, this book is an efficient and handy resource that enables you to resolve a problem quickly and without recourse to complicated, time-consuming, or expensive solutions.

How This Book Is Organized

This book isn't meant to be read from cover to cover (although, of course, you're free to do so if you wish). Instead, most of the book divides iOS troubleshooting into a number of targeted categories, which I hope will make it easy for you to locate the particular problem you want to prevent, solve, or work around.

To help you find your way around, here's a summary of the book's dozen chapters:

- **Chapter 1, "Learning Some General Troubleshooting Techniques"** — This chapter takes you through a few useful techniques for troubleshooting most problems. If you don't see a specific fix for a problem you're having, try one or more of the general solutions in this chapter.

- **Chapter 2, "Fixing Networking and Cellular Woes"** — This chapter focuses on connectivity problems, especially those related to the cellular network and to Wi-Fi networks.

- **Chapter 3, "Solving App Problems"** — This chapter looks at troubles related to apps, such as having an app freeze on you.

- **Chapter 4, "Resolving Web Issues"** — This chapter concentrates on problems related to use the Safari app to surf the Web and to search for information.

- **Chapter 5, "Overcoming Email Glitches"** — This chapter tackles the Mail app and takes you through a number of problems related to sending and receiving email.

- **Chapter 6, "Fixing Phone Troubles"** — If you have an iPhone, this chapter looks at issues that might arise when receiving or making phone calls, as well as other problems related to the Phone app.

- **Chapter 7, "Solving Problems Related to Cameras and Photos"** — This chapter focuses (pun intended) on problems related to using both the Camera app to capture images, and the Photos app to process those images.

- **Chapter 8, "Protecting Your Device"** — This chapter shows you how to keep your iOS device safe by running through a few preventative maintenance tasks such as locking your device, backing up your data, and finding and protecting a lost device.

- **Chapter 9, "Solving Privacy Problems"** — This chapter takes a detailed look at how you can maintain privacy when you use iOS, including both general privacy issues and concerns related to web browsing privacy.

- **Chapter 10, "Repairing Battery and Charging Problems"** — This chapter looks at problems related to the device battery, including tracking battery use and extending battery life.

- **Chapter 11, "Getting Around Accessibility Issues"** — This chapter concentrates on configuring iOS to work around challenges related to visual, physical, and aural impairments or disabilities.

- **Chapter 12, "Troubleshooting Other iOS Problems"** — This chapter completes the book with a miscellany of troubleshooting tools, techniques, and workarounds for a variety of problems that didn't fit into any of the other chapters.

Features of This Book

To help you get the most of the book and to make your troubleshooting chores more efficient, this book includes the following features:

- Throughout the book, I've broken many of the troubleshooting procedures and workarounds into easy-to-follow, step-by-step procedures.

- Jargon-free explanations of key concepts

- Extensive use of screenshots to illustrate many of the book's procedures

- Tips, tricks, and shortcuts to make troubleshooting your iOS device easier and faster

- A friendly and lightly humorous tone that I hope will help you feel at home with the subject and keep boredom at bay

This book also uses the following boxes to draw your attention to important (or merely interesting) information:

Note   The Note box presents asides that give you more information about the current troubleshooting topic. These tidbits provide extra insights that offer a better understanding of the task.

Tip   The Tip box tells you about methods that are easier, faster, or more efficient than the standard methods.

Caution   The all-important Caution box tells you about potential accidents waiting to happen. There are always ways to mess things up when you're working with iOS. These boxes help you avoid those traps and pitfalls.

CHAPTER 1

Learning Some General Troubleshooting Techniques

When you're using a computer — particularly a Windows PC, but also a Mac — there's a weird nervousness that operates just below the surface of your awareness. That trepidation comes from experience: your computer almost certainly has crashed not only many times in the past, but also some time recently. So in a sense you're just *waiting* for things to go south because you know they eventually will.

When you're using your iPhone, iPad, or other iOS device, that underlying unease is nowhere to be found. This blissfully anxiety-free state also comes from experience: your iOS device almost never crashes, so you're not expecting it to. Notice, however, that I said *almost* never. The reality is that, although they occur far less frequently than with Windows or macOS, iOS problems *do* occur. That shouldn't come as a surprise because the iPhone, iPad, and iPod touch are extremely sophisticated devices — they're full-blown computers, really. And any sophisticated device will always have problems, thanks to its sheer complexity. Fortunately, iOS devices have fewer moving parts than regular computers, so overall there's less to go wrong with the hardware. You also see fewer problems on the software side because app developers only have to build their products to work with a relatively small collection of devices, all of which are manufactured by a single company. This really simplifies things, and the result is fewer problems. Again, however, not zero problems.

To help you troubleshoot any hardware or software glitches that come up, this chapter offers you some general troubleshooting techniques that apply to all iOS devices: the iPhone, the iPad, and the iPod touch.

Restarting and Rebooting

If your iOS device is behaving oddly or erratically, it's possible that a specific component inside the device is the cause. In that case, you don't have much choice but to leave your device at the Genius Bar, or ship it back to Apple for repairs. Fortunately, however, most glitches are temporary and can often be fixed by employing a few standard techniques, particularly restarting or rebooting your device.

© Paul McFedries 2017
P. McFedries, *Troubleshooting iOS*, DOI 10.1007/978-1-4842-2445-8_1

If your iPhone is behaving oddly or erratically, it's possible that a specific component inside the phone is the cause. In that case, you don't have much choice but to ship your iPhone back to Apple for repairs. Fortunately, however, most glitches are temporary and can often be fixed by using one or more of the following techniques:

Restarting Your Device

By far the most common solution to an iOS device problem is to shut it down and then restart it. By rebooting the device, you reset the entire system, which is often enough to solve many problems.

You restart an iOS device using the Sleep/Wake button, the location of which depends on your device:

- For the iPhone 6 and later, the button appears on the right edge of the phone, near the top.

- For all other iOS devices, the button appears on the top edge of the device, toward the right side.

Press and hold the Sleep/Wake button for a few seconds until you see the Slide to Power Off screen (at which point you can release the button). Drag the Slide to Power Off slider to the right to start the shutdown. When the screen goes completely black, your device is off. To restart, press and hold the Sleep/Wake button until you see the Apple logo and then release the button.

Rebooting Your Device Hardware

When you restart your iOS device by pressing and holding Sleep/Wake for a few seconds, what you're really doing is rebooting the system software. If that still doesn't solve the problem, you might need to reboot the device hardware as well. To do that, press and hold down the Sleep/Wake and Home buttons at the same time. Keep them pressed until you see the Apple logo (it takes about 8 seconds or so), which indicates a successful restart.

■ **Note**   A hardware reboot is also the way to go if your iOS device is *really* stuck and holding down just the Sleep/Wake button doesn't do anything. It happens.

Updating Software

iOS checks for available updates from time to time when it's connected to the Internet. If an update is available, you see a badge on the Settings app icon, as shown in Figure 1-1. You might also see a Software Update notification telling you that a new version of iOS is ready to install.

Figure 1-1. *When iOS detects that an update is available, it alerts you with a badge on the Settings app icon*

To proceed with the update, follow these steps:

1. If the Software Update alert is displayed, tap Install Now. Otherwise, on the Home screen, tap Settings. The Settings app appears.

2. Tap General. iOS displays the General screen. As you can see in Figure 1-2, when an update is available, you also see badges on the General tab and the Software Update command.

Figure 1-2. *When an update is ready for you, iOS displays badges on the Settings app's General tab and Software Update command*

3. Tap Download and Install. iOS downloads the update and then proceeds with the installation, which takes a few minutes.

Caution

■ **Note**   Your iOS device only goes through with the update if it will have more than 50-percent battery life through the entire update operation. To ensure the update is a success, either plug your device into an AC outlet or only run the update when the battery is fully charged.

Restoring Your Device from a Backup

It's often the case that simply changing a setting or adding an app or some data can cause your iOS device to act wonky. Ideally the fix would be to return the setting to its previous state or remove the app or data, but it's not always obvious which setting or bit of content is the culprit.

One solution is to return your device to an earlier state by restoring a recent backup. If you go back far enough, you should restore to a state in which the problem doesn't exist. (Ideally, you shouldn't go back any further than necessary because then you run too great a risk of losing other settings, apps, and data.)

Follow these steps to restore a recent backup:

1. On your device, turn off Find My iPhone, if it's turned on. You do this by opening Settings, tapping iCloud, tapping Find My *Device* (where *Device* is iPhone, iPad or iPod), tapping the Find My *Device* switch to Off, and then entering your Apple password.

2. Connect your device to your computer.

3. In iTunes, click the device icon.

4. Click the Summary tab.

5. Click Restore Backup. iTunes asks you to select a backup to restore, as shown in Figure 1-3.

Figure 1-3. *Select an earlier backup that was made before you began experiencing problems on your device*

6. Select the older backup that you want to restore. This should be the most recent backup that was made before the problem first occurred.

7. Click Restore. iTunes restores the backup and restarts the device.

Restoring Factory Settings

Sometimes your iOS device goes down for the count because its settings have become corrupted. In that case, you can fix the problem by restoring the device to its default factory settings.

Restoring Factory Defaults Via iTunes

The best way to restore factory settings is to use the Restore feature in iTunes because that enables you to back up and restore any settings you've changed on the device. There are a couple of things to think about here:

- If the corrupted setting is an iOS default that you never changed, then the restore operation will overwrite that corrupted setting and your problem should be solved. In that case, you should back up and restore your own settings.

- If the corrupted setting is one that you changed, then backing up and restoring your settings will likely re-create the problem. In that case, you should *not* back up and restore your settings.

So what route should you take? First, try running the restore procedure by backing up and restoring your settings. If the problem goes away, you're set; if the problem recurs, then it means one of your changed settings is the culprit, so you should repeat the restore, but this time don't back up your settings.

Before proceeding, note that these steps require that your device be able to connect to your computer and be visible in iTunes. If that's not the case, see the instructions for resetting the device in the next section. Otherwise, follow these steps to restore your device:

1. On your device, turn off Find My iPhone, if it's turned on. You do this by opening Settings, tapping iCloud, tapping Find My *Device* (where *Device* is iPhone, iPad, or iPod), tapping the Find My *Device* switch to Off, and then entering your Apple password.

2. Connect your device to your computer.

3. In iTunes, click the device icon.

4. Click the Summary tab.

5. Click Back Up Now. This ensures that iTunes has a backup copy of your device data and settings.

▪ **Caution**   By default, iTunes doesn't back up sensitive information such as saved passwords, web site history, and health data. To back up that data, select the Encrypt *device* backup check box (where *device* is iPhone, iPad, or iPod) and then run the backup.

---

6. Click Restore *Device* (where *Device* is iPhone, iPad, or iPod). iTunes asks you to confirm you want to restore.

7. Click Restore and then follow the prompts on the screen. iTunes downloads iOS and restores the original settings. When your device restarts, iTunes connects to it and might ask you to enter your Apple ID credentials. After you've done that, iTunes displays the Welcome to Your New *device* screen, as shown in Figure 1-4.

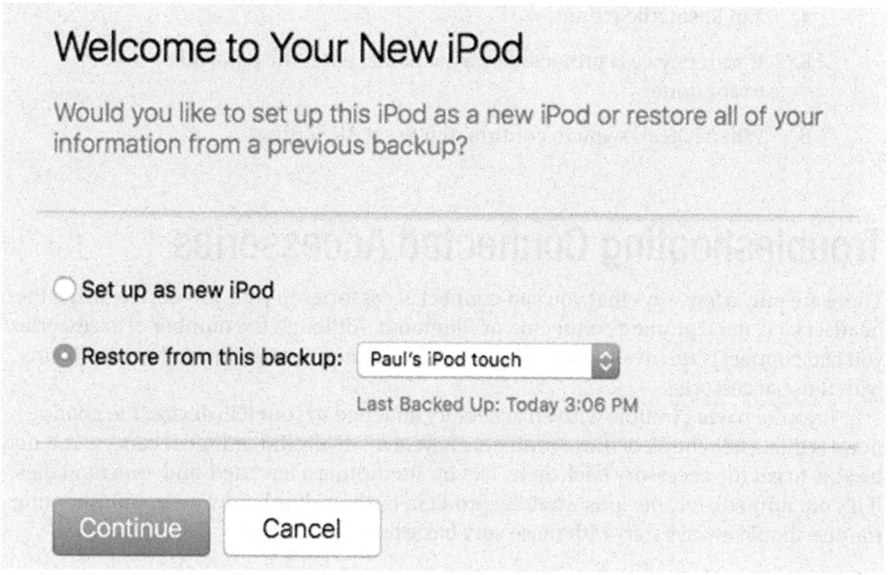

Welcome to Your New iPod

Would you like to set up this iPod as a new iPod or restore all of your information from a previous backup?

○ Set up as new iPod

◉ Restore from this backup: | Paul's iPod touch | ⬍ |

Last Backed Up: Today 3:06 PM

| Continue | Cancel |

Figure 1-4. *When your factory-fresh device restarts, iTunes offers to restore your backed-up settings and data*

8. Select the Restore from this backup option.

9. If you happen to have more than one device backed up, use the list to choose yours.

10. Click Continue. iTunes restores your backed-up data, restarts your device, and syncs it.

11. Go through the tabs and check the sync settings to make sure they're set up the way you want.

12. If you made any changes to the settings, click Apply. This ensures that your device has all its data restored.

Restoring Factory Settings on the Device

If your device is having problems that prevent it from connecting to your computer or being recognized by iTunes, you can still restore the factory default settings directly on the device. Here are the steps to follow:

1. Tap Settings in the Home screen.

2. Tap General.

3. Tap Reset.

7

4.   Tap Reset All Settings.

5.   If your device is protected by a passcode, enter the passcode
     to continue.

6.   When iOS asks you to confirm, tap Reset All Settings.

Troubleshooting Connected Accessories

There are only a few ways that you can connect accessories to your iOS device: using the headset jack, the Lightning connector, or Bluetooth. Although the number of accessories you can connect is relatively limited, that doesn't mean you might never have problems with those accessories .

If you're having trouble with an accessory attached to your iOS device, the good news is that a fair chunk of those problems have a relatively limited set of causes. You may be able to get the accessory back on its feet by attempting a few tried-and-true remedies. If it's not immediately obvious what the problem is, then your hardware troubleshooting routine should always start with these very basic techniques:

- **Check connections, power switches, and so on.** Some of the most common (and most embarrassing) causes of hardware problems are the simple physical things, so make sure that the connected accessory is turned on and check that the cables (if any) are seated properly. For example, if you can't access the Internet through the Wi-Fi connection on your iOS device, make sure your network's router is turned on. Also make sure that the cable between your router and the ISP's modem (if they aren't a single device, as is often the case these days) is properly connected.

- **Replace the batteries.** Wireless devices such as headsets really chew through batteries, so if such a device is working intermittently (or not at all), always try replacing the batteries to see if that solves the problem.

- **Turn the accessory off and then on again.** You *power cycle* a device by turning it off, waiting a few seconds for its innards to stop spinning, and then turning it back on. You'd be amazed how often this simple procedure can get a device back up and running. For a device that doesn't have an On/Off switch, try either unplugging it from the power outlet or removing and replacing the batteries.

- **Reset the accessory's default settings.** If you can configure the accessory, then perhaps some new setting is causing the problem. If you recently made a change, try returning the setting back to its original value. If that doesn't do the trick, most configurable devices have some kind of Restore Default Settings option that enables you to quickly return them to their factory settings.

- **Upgrade the accessory's firmware.** Some devices come with *firmware* — a small program that runs inside the device and controls its internal functions. For example, all routers have firmware. Check with the manufacturer to see if a new version exists. If it does, download the new version and then see the device's manual to learn how to upgrade the firmware.

Advanced Troubleshooting Techniques

The techniques you've seen so far will in many cases get your iOS device back up and running. If not, there are still a couple of other techniques you can try.

Restoring Factory Settings When You Can't Launch iOS

In some rare cases, your iOS device goes utterly haywire, where not only does iTunes not recognize the device, but you can't even launch iOS. If this happens, you can still recover everything, but you have to do it using a special hardware mode called Device Firmware Upgrade (DFU). This mode essentially bypasses the current OS installed on the phone (which is good because in this scenario your current OS is toast) and tells iTunes to install a factory-fresh version of iOS. You can then restore your stuff as described earlier in this chapter (see "Restoring Your Device from a Backup").

Follow these steps to put your device into DFU mode:

1. Turn off your device.

2. Connect your device to your Mac or your Windows PC.

3. Launch iTunes.

4. Press and hold down the Sleep/Wake and Home buttons for exactly 10 seconds.

5. After 10 seconds, release the Sleep/Wake button, but continue to hold down the Home button for another 10 seconds.

6.   After 10 seconds, release the Home button. iTunes now recognizes your device and displays the dialog shown in Figure 1-5.

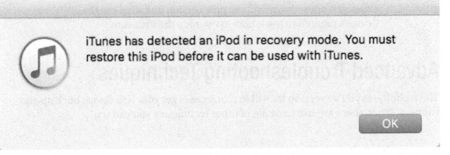

iTunes has detected an iPod in recovery mode. You must restore this iPod before it can be used with iTunes.

OK

Figure 1-5. *When you boot your iOS device in DFU mode, iTunes recognizes the device and displays this dialog to remind you to restore it*

7.   Click OK.

8.   Click Restore *Device* (where *device* is iPhone, iPad, or iPod). iTunes asks you to confirm you want to restore.

9.   Click Restore and Update. iTunes downloads and installs iOS and then restores your device to the factory defaults.

Erasing Your Device

If restoring the factory settings doesn't get the job done, it could be some recalcitrant bit of content that's causing the problem. In that case, you need to reset not only all your iOS settings, but all your content, as well. Here's how it's done:

1.   Tap Settings.

2.   Tap General.

3.   Tap Reset.

4.   Tap Reset All Content and Settings.

5.   Enter your device passcode, if it's set.

6.   When iOS asks you to confirm, tap Erase *Device* (where *Device* is iPhone, iPad, or iPod).

■ **Caution**   Unless you really do want to start over with original settings and no content, only run the Erase All Content and Settings command if you have your device backed up. See Chapter 8, "Protecting Your Device."

CHAPTER 2

▪ ▪ ▪

Fixing Networking and Cellular Woes

Your iOS device lets you perform a satisfyingly large range of fun and interesting tasks while you're offline. You can play games, read saved articles, listen to downloaded music or podcasts, crack open an e-book, update your contacts, and much more. But iOS and the iPhone, iPad, and iPod touch really shine when they have access to the outside world, either via a Wi-Fi network or a cellular signal. With a link established, you can surf, e-mail, message, post, upload, download, and perform all the other online verbs that are the watchwords of today's connected lifestyle.

Alas, you might find yourself having to revert to the satisfying-but-limited world of offline pastimes if you have trouble connecting your iOS device to a network. Even if you can get online, iOS might still cause you grief with the way it handles network or cellular connections. This chapter takes you through quite a few connectivity problems and offers solutions that will help you get iOS and your network working smoothly again.

Troubleshooting Wi-Fi Issues

If your network has become a "notwork" (some wags also refer to a downed network as a nyetwork), this chapter offers a few solutions that might help. I don't make any claim to completeness here, however; after all, most network ills are a combination of several factors and therefore are relatively obscure and difficult to reproduce. Instead, I just go through a few general strategies for tracking down problems and pose solutions for some of the most common network afflictions.

You Have Trouble Accessing a Wi-Fi Network: Part I

If you're having trouble connecting to a local Wi-Fi network, the problem might be with your device or it might be with the network itself. (I'm assuming here that you have a password for the network, if it requires one.) Let's begin here in Part I by assuming that the problem rests with your device.

© Paul McFedries 2017
P. McFedries, *Troubleshooting iOS*, DOI 10.1007/978-1-4842-2445-8_2

Solution: Turn the Wi-Fi antenna off and then on again. This resets the antenna, which is often enough to make the connection go through. To toggle the antenna, open Settings, tap Wi-Fi, tap the Wi-Fi switch (see Figure 2-1) to Off, and then tap the same switch back to On.

■ **Tip** You can also toggle the Wi-Fi antenna off and on by swiping up from the bottom of the screen to open the Control Center and then tapping the Wi-Fi icon twice. Tap outside the Control Center to close it.

Wi-Fi

Wi-Fi

Figure 2-1. Toggling the W-Fi switch off and then on again can often solve Wi-Fi woes

You Have Trouble Accessing a Wi-Fi Network: Part II

If your iOS device still won't connect to the Wi-Fi hotspot, then it's possible the problem lies with the network itself. Unfortunately, wireless networking adds a whole new set of potential snags to your troubleshooting chores because of problems such as interference, compatibility, and device ranges.

Solution: Here's a list of a few troubleshooting items that you should check to solve any wireless connectivity problems you're having:

- **Reboot devices.** Reset your hardware by turning off the Wi-Fi network's router and then turning it back on again. If your network has a separate broadband modem, you should reboot that as well.

- **Look for interference.** Devices such as baby monitors and cordless phones that use the 2.4GHz radio frequency (RF) band can play havoc with wireless signals. Try either moving or turning off such devices if they're near your wireless router.

■ **Caution** You should also keep your wireless router well away from a microwave oven; microwaves can jam wireless signals.

- **Check your range.** If you're getting no signal or a weak signal, it could be that your iOS device is too far away from the Wi-Fi router. You usually can't get much farther than about 115 feet away from any Wi-Fi access point before the signal begins to degrade (230 feet if you're using 802.11n devices). Either move closer to the router, or turn on the router's range booster feature, if it has one. You could also install a wireless range extender.

- **Change the channel.** You can configure your wireless router to broadcast signals on a specific channel. Sometimes one channel gives a stronger signal than another, so try changing the channel. You do this by logging on to the router's configuration pages and looking for a setting that determines the broadcast channel.

- **Upgrade the router's firmware.** Some network problems are caused by router bugs. If the manufacturer has corrected these bugs, the fixes will appear in the latest version of the router firmware, so you should upgrade to the new version. See your router documentation to learn how to perform an upgrade.

- **Reset the router.** As a last resort, reset the router to its default factory settings (see the device documentation to learn how to do this). Note if you do this you'll need to set up your network from scratch.

iOS Automatically Connects to a Network You No Longer Want to Use

When you join a Wi-Fi network, iOS remembers your connection details and joins that network automatically the next time it comes within range. This is convenient for networks you want to use, but it's a pain for networks you no longer need. A common dilemma is having multiple networks available, one of which is more desirable (because, say, it's faster or cheaper). If you've previously connected to some or all of the other networks, then there's a good chance iOS will choose one of them for its automatic connection, leaving you with the hassle of connecting to the network you want manually.

Solution: Tell iOS to forget the network (or networks) you don't want to use:

1. Run the Settings app and then tap Wi-Fi to open the Wi-Fi Networks screen.

2. Tap the blue More Info icon to the right of the network you want to forget. iOS displays the network's settings screen.

3. Tap Forget this Network, shown in Figure 2-2. iOS asks you to confirm.

4. Tap Forget. iOS discards the login data for the network and no longer connects to the network automatically.

Figure 2-2. *If you no longer want to connect to a particular network, tap the Forget This Network button*

You're Getting Frequent Prompts to Join Nearby Wi-Fi Networks

By default, when your device requires a network connection and you're not already connected to a Wi-Fi network, iOS displays the Select a Wireless Network dialog to show you nearby networks. However, as you move around town, you may find that dialog popping up all too frequently as new Wi-Fi networks come within range (although iOS is smart enough not to prompt when you're moving quickly — such as when you're driving). These constant prompts are both annoying and inconvenient.

Solution: Tell iOS to stop prompting you to join nearby networks. Open the Settings app, tap Wi-Fi, and then tap the Ask to Join Networks switch to Off, as shown in Figure 2-3.

Figure 2-3. *To turn off the constant prompts to join nearby Wi-Fi networks, tap the Ask to Join Networks switch to Off*

You Want to Connect to a Hidden Wi-Fi Network

Each Wi-Fi network has a network name — often called the *Service Set Identifier*, or *SSID* — which identifies the network to Wi-Fi devices. By default, Wi-Fi networks broadcast the network name so that you can see it in the Select a Wireless Network dialog or the Wi-Fi screen in the Settings app. However, some Wi-Fi networks disable network name broadcasting as a security precaution. Why? The thinking is that if an unauthorized user can't see the network, he or she can't attempt to connect to it. (However, some devices can still pick up the network name when authorized computers connect to it, so this is not a foolproof security measure.) If you're an authorized user, however, how do you connect to a network you can't see?

Solution: You can connect to a hidden Wi-Fi network by entering the connection settings by hand. You need to know the network name, its security and encryption types, and the network password. Here's how it's done:

1. Open the Settings app and then tap Wi-Fi.

2. In the list of nearby networks, tap Other. iOS displays the Other Network screen.

3. Type the network name in the Name text box.

4. Tap Security to open the Security screen and then tap the type of security the Wi-Fi network uses: None, WEP, WPA, WPA2, WPA Enterprise, or WPA2 Enterprise. If you're not sure, most secure networks use WPA2.

5. Tap Other Network to return to the Other Network screen. If you chose WEP, WPA, WPA2, WPA Enterprise, or WPA2 Enterprise, iOS prompts you to enter the network password.

6. Type the password in the Password text box, as shown in Figure 2-4.

7. Tap Join. iOS connects to the network.

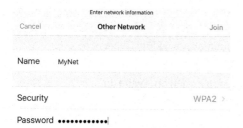

Figure 2-4. *To join a hidden network, type the network name, select the security type, and then enter the password*

You're Having Trouble Sending a File via AirDrop

You can transfer files between your Mac and your iOS device by syncing via iTunes. However, if you just want to pass along a single file from your device to the other, the sync procedure is overkill. Instead, if your Mac is running OS X Yosemite or later and your iPhone is running iOS 8 or later, and your Mac and iPhone are connected to the same Wi-Fi network, you can use a tool called AirDrop to send a file directly between your Mac and your device.

However, you might find that the two devices don't see each other or that the file does not transfer.

Solution: If you don't see your iOS device from your Mac, or if you don't see your Mac from your iOS device, here are some things to check:

- Make sure that both your Mac and your iOS device are connected to the same Wi-Fi network.

- AirDrop requires Bluetooth as well as Wi-Fi, so make sure both your Mac and your iOS device have Bluetooth enabled:

  - In iOS, swipe up from the bottom of the screen to display the Control Center, and then tap to activate the Bluetooth icon. Tap outside the Control Center to close it.

  - In macOS (or OS X), open System Preferences, click Bluetooth, and then make sure the Bluetooth setting is On. (If it says Off, click Turn Bluetooth On.)

■ **Tip**   If you have Wi-Fi and/or Bluetooth turned off in iOS, a quick way to turn them both on is to open any share sheet and tap the AirDrop icon. You can also swipe up from the bottom of the screen to display the Control Center, tap AirDrop, and then tap Contacts Only. Tap outside the Control Center to close it.

- Make sure your iOS device and your Mac are within 33 feet of each other so that they can discover each other via Bluetooth.

- Make sure the iOS device has AirDrop turned on. Swipe up from the bottom of the screen to display the Control Center, tap AirDrop, and then tap Contacts Only (see Figure 2-5). If you still don't see your device on your Mac, tap Everyone, instead.

Figure 2-5. In the iOS Control Center, tap AirDrop and then tap either Contacts Only or Everyone

- Make sure your Mac is discoverable. Open the AirDrop window (in Finder, click Go and then click AirDrop, or press Shift+Cmd+R). In the Allow me to be discovered by list, select Contacts Only. If you still don't see your Mac from iOS, select Everyone, instead.

- If you've set AirDrop to Contacts Only, make sure both your iOS device and your Mac are signed in to the same iCloud account.

- Make sure neither your iOS device nor your Mac are in sleep mode.

If an AirDrop file transfer fails, try these solutions:

- Make sure neither your iOS device nor your Mac are in Do Not Disturb mode:

  - In iOS, swipe up from the bottom of the screen to display the Control Center, and then tap to deactivate the Do Not Disturb icon.

  - In OS X or macOS, click the Notifications icon to display the Notification Center, click the Notifications tab, scroll to the top of the tab, and then click to set the Do Not Disturb switch to Off.

- Make sure your iOS device doesn't have the Personal Hotspot feature activated. Open the Settings app, tap Personal Hotspot, and then tap the Personal Hotspot switch to Off.

- Do not try to send multiple files of different file types. For example, while it's okay to send two or more image files, you can't send, say, an image file and a PDF at the same time.

- Make sure your Mac isn't in legacy mode, where it's configured to only send files to Macs issued in 2012 or earlier. On the Mac, open the AirDrop window. If you see the text "Searching for older Macs...," click Cancel to exit legacy mode.

- Make sure the Mac Firewall isn't configured to block all incoming connections. Open System Preferences, click Security & Privacy, click Firewall, click the lock icon, and then enter your Mac's administrative password. Click to deactivate the Block all incoming connections check box, if necessary, and then click OK.

If all else fails, reset your iOS network settings. In the Settings app, tap General, tap Reset, tap Reset Network Settings, and then when iOS asks you to confirm, tap Reset Network Settings.

Troubleshooting Cellular Issues

If you have an iPhone or an iPad with a cellular antenna, you know the freedom and efficiency of having an always-on data connection as long as there's a cellular network within range. That convenience doesn't come cheap, unfortunately, so most cellular problems center around keeping your data and roaming charges in check. This section takes you through these and other cellular-related problems.

You Can Send E-Mail over Wi-Fi but Not over Cellular

You might find that you can send e-mail messages just fine at home or at work, but e-mails sent while you're walking around town or in transit just sit in the Mail app's Outbox. This feels like a bug, but it's actually a feature because many cellular providers don't allow mail to be sent through third-party servers. That's not a problem when you're on Wi-Fi because your messages don't get sent via the cellular network, but as soon as you're off Wi-Fi, the cellular network kicks in and your provider prevents third-party messages from being sent.

Solution: Your cellular provider will have set up an outgoing server to handle sent messages, so you need to set up that server as a secondary SMTP server for your e-mail account. iOS will try sending messages using the account's default server, but if that fails (when you're on the cellular network instead of a Wi-Fi network, for example), it will fall back to the secondary server and your message will get sent.

To set up a secondary SMTP server, follow these steps:

1. Open the Settings app and then tap Mail, Contacts, Calendars.

2. Tap your e-mail account.

3. Tap your outgoing mail server.

4. Tap Add Server.

5. Enter your cellular provider's SMTP host name, as well as your user name and password.

6. Tap Save.

You Are Not Sure How Much Data You Are Using

If you're using your iOS device with a plan that comes with a maximum amount of monthly data and you exceed that monthly cap, you'll almost certainly pay big bucks for the privilege. To avoid that, most cellular providers are kind enough to send you a message when you approach your cap. However, if you don't trust that process, or if you're just paranoid about these things (justly, in my view), then you might prefer to keep an eye on your data usage yourself.

Solution: iOS keeps track of the cellular network data it has sent or received, as well as the roaming data it has sent or received if you've used your iPhone out of your coverage area. First, take a look at your most recent bill from your cellular provider and, in particular, look for the dates the bill covers. For example, the bill might run from the 24th of one month to the 23rd of the next month. This is important because it tells you when you need to reset the usage data on your device.

Now follow these steps to check your cellular data usage:

1. Open the Settings app and then tap Cellular to display the Cellular screen.

2. In the Cellular Data Usage section, read the Current Period and Current Period Roaming values (see Figure 2-6).

3. If you're at the end of your data period, tap Reset Statistics at the bottom of the screen to start with fresh values for the new period.

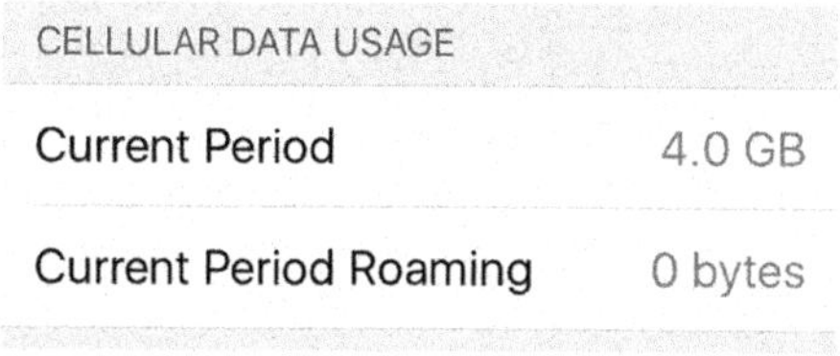

CELLULAR DATA USAGE	
Current Period	4.0 GB
Current Period Roaming	0 bytes

Figure 2-6. *Read the values in the Cellular Data Usage section*

You Want to Prevent Your iOS Device from Using Cellular Data

If you've reached the limit of your cellular data plan, you almost certainly want to avoid going over the cap because the charges are usually prohibitively expensive. As long as you have a Wi-Fi network in range, or you're disciplined enough not to surf the Web or cruise YouTube when there's no Wi-Fi in sight, you'll be okay. Still, accidents can happen. For example, you might accidentally tap a link in an e-mail message or text message, or someone in your household might use your phone without knowing about your restrictions.

Solution: To prevent these sorts of accidents (or if you simply don't trust yourself when it comes to YouTube), you can turn off cellular data altogether, which means your device accesses Internet data only if it has a Wi-Fi signal. To turn off cellular data on your iOS device, open the Settings app, tap Cellular, and then tap the Cellular Data switch to Off.

You Want More Control over How Your iOS Device Uses Cellular Data

Rather than turning off cellular data completely, as I described in the previous section, you can take a more targeted approach. For example, if you're a bit worried about going over your cellular plan's data ceiling, it makes sense to avoid relatively high-bandwidth items, such as FaceTime and iTunes, but not relatively low-bandwidth content, such as iCloud documents and the Safari reading list.

Solution: You could just police this yourself but, hey, you're a busy person and you might forget the next time a FaceTime call comes in and you're in a cellular-only neighborhood. I say leave the details to iOS by configuring it to not allow certain content types over a cellular connection. To do that, open the Settings app and tap Cellular. In the Use Cellular Data For section, shown in Figure 2-7, tap the switch to Off for each type of content you want to ban from cellular.

USE CELLULAR DATA FOR:

Adobe Acrobat 108 KB		
Alarm Clock 3.1 MB		
Anki 20.9 KB		
App Store 75.1 MB		
Audible 1.2 MB		

Figure 2-7. *Tap the switch to Off beside each app you want to keep off your cellular connection*

You Want to Prevent iOS from Using Data Roaming

Data roaming is an often-convenient feature that enables you to make calls — and, with your iOS device, surf the Web, check and send e-mail, and exchange text messages — when you're outside of your normal coverage area. The downside is that, unless you've got a fixed-rate roaming package from your cellular provider, roaming charges are almost always eye-poppingly expensive. You're often talking several dollars per minute or megabyte, depending on where you are and what type of service you're using. Not good!

Unfortunately, if you have the iOS Data Roaming feature turned on, you may incur massive roaming charges even if you never use your device! That's because iOS still performs background checks for things like incoming e-mail messages and text messages, so a week in some far-off land could cost you hundreds of dollars without even using your phone.

Solution: To avoid this, turn off the Data Roaming feature on your device when you don't need it. To do this, open the Settings app, tap Cellular, tap Cellular Data Options, and then tap the Data Roaming switch to Off.

Troubleshooting Bluetooth Issues

iOS supports a wireless technology called Bluetooth, which enables you to make wireless connections to other Bluetooth-friendly devices, such as headsets, keyboards, and game controllers. In theory, connecting Bluetooth devices is supposed be criminally easy, but in practice that's often not the case, so this section provides you with a few common troubleshooting techniques.

You Don't See a Bluetooth Device

Not surprisingly, you can't make a Bluetooth connection if you can't see the device in the Settings app's Bluetooth window.

Solution: If you don't see a Bluetooth device in the Settings app, try the following:

- Make sure the device is turned on and fully charged.

- Make sure the device is discoverable. Unlike Wi-Fi devices that broadcast their signals constantly, most Bluetooth devices broadcast their availability — that is, they make themselves *discoverable* — only when you say so. Most Bluetooth devices have a switch you can turn on or a button you can press to make them discoverable.

- Make sure the Bluetooth device is well within 33 feet of your iOS device, since that's the maximum range for most Bluetooth devices. (Some so-called *Class 1* Bluetooth devices have a maximum range 10 times as long.)

- Make sure iOS has Bluetooth enabled. In the Settings app, tap Bluetooth, and then tap the Bluetooth switch to On, as shown in Figure 2-8.

Figure 2-8. *In the Settings app, make sure the Bluetooth switch is set to On*

- If possible, reboot the Bluetooth device. If you can't reboot the device, or the reboot doesn't solve the problem, reboot your iOS device.

- Check with the Bluetooth device manufacturer to ensure the device is capable of being paired with iOS devices.

You Can't Pair with a Bluetooth Device

As a security precaution, many Bluetooth devices need to be paired with another device before the connection is established. In some cases, the pairing is accomplished by entering a multidigit passkey — iOS calls it a PIN — that you must then enter into the Bluetooth device (assuming, of course, that it has some kind of keypad). For all other Bluetooth devices, you initiate the pairing by tapping the device in the Settings app's Bluetooth screen. Either way, you might find that even though the device shows up fine in the Bluetooth screen, you cannot pair it with your iOS device.

Solution: First try the solutions in the previous section. If you still can't get the pairing to work, tell iOS to start over by forgetting what it knows about the device:

1. Open the Settings app, and then tap Bluetooth.

2. Tap the blue More Info icon to the right of the Bluetooth device name.

3. Tap Forget this Device. iOS asks you to confirm.

4. Tap OK.

5. When the device reappears in the Bluetooth window, trying pairing with it again.

You Don't Hear Audio through a Paired Headset

After you pair a Bluetooth headset, iOS is usually smart enough to start blasting your tunes through the headset instead of the device's built-in speaker. The operative word here is "usually," since every so often iOS fails to do this.

Solution: You need to manually specify your paired headset as the output device. Swipe up from the bottom of the screen to open the Control Center, tap the AirPlay icon that appears below the playback controls (to the right of the AirDrop section), and then tap your paired Bluetooth headset (see Figure 2-9). iOS now plays your device audio through the headset.

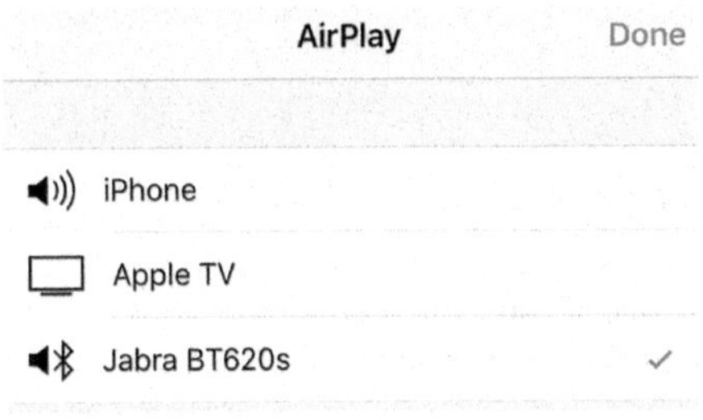

Figure 2-9. *Open the AirPlay screen and then tap your paired Bluetooth headset*

CHAPTER 3

■ ■ ■

Solving App Problems

Your iPhone, iPad, or iPod touch is an impressive piece of industrial design. From the responsive touchscreen to the powerful cameras to the overall sleek design, an iOS device is a work of art as much as it's a work of engineering. But all that hardware is useless without some software to make it come alive, and in the iOS world, that software comes in the form of the app. This includes not only the various apps that are installed by default with iOS, but also those Apple and third-party apps that are available for download using the App Store.

In short, world-class hardware notwithstanding, your iOS device is both defined and constrained by the apps that are installed on it. Why constrained? Because it's the stark truth that if your apps don't work properly, then neither does your iOS device. If you can't find an app, if an app crashes, or if an app behaves in a way the developer didn't intend, then your iOS experience will be compromised. To help you avoid that situation — or to help you get out of it — this chapter presents a few problems and solutions related to apps.

General App Troubleshooting

App problems can run the gamut from not being able to locate an app or its data (bothersome), to an app behaving strangely (annoying), or to an app not working at all (aggravating). The good news is that, unless the app was created by a truly incompetent developer, most app problems can be solved quickly or, at least, straightforwardly.

You Find Searching Difficult Because iOS Returns Items from Too Many Apps

When you run a Spotlight search on your iOS device, you might see results from a wide variety of apps, depending on the search text. For a more general search, you can easily see results from a couple of dozen or more apps.

© Paul McFedries 2017
P. McFedries, *Troubleshooting iOS*, DOI 10.1007/978-1-4842-2445-8_3

Solution: Configure Spotlight search to not show results from apps you use only rarely or from apps you never search. To configure Spotlight search, open the Settings app, tap General, and then tap Spotlight Search. In the Search Results section, tap the switch to Off beside each app you want to exclude from the search (see Figure 3-1).

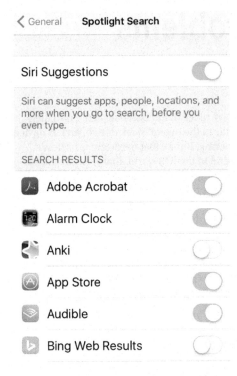

Figure 3-1. In Settings, use the Spotlight Search screen to tell iOS which apps to exclude from the search results

You Find It Difficult to Locate an App

If you get a bit carried away at the App Store, you can easily end up with a couple of hundred icons scattered over a dozen or more pages (the max is 15 pages). Since the apps were most likely installed in no particular order, finding a single app icon can be frustratingly time consuming.

Solution: You can reset your Home screen layout, which does two things:

- It restores the main Home screen and possibly part of the second Home screen (depending on the device and iOS version) to the factory default icon arrangement.

- It displays all your third-party app icons in alphabetical order.

■ **Caution**   Resetting the Home screen layout also deletes any custom app folders that you created.

To reset your Home screen layout, open Settings, tap General, tap Reset, tap Reset Home Screen Layout, and then when iOS asks for confirmation, tap Reset Home Screen.

An App Is Displaying Too Many Notifications

Like a noisy or rude houseguest, some apps respond to being invited into your iOS home by displaying notifications that are too frequent or too insistent.

Solution: Take control of the app's notifications by configuring them to your liking. Open the Settings app, tap Notifications, and then tap the app you want to work with. iOS displays the app's notification options, as shown in Figure 3-2. Note that some apps — such as Calendar — divide their notifications into categories, so you might need to tap a category before you see options such as those shown in Figure 3-2.

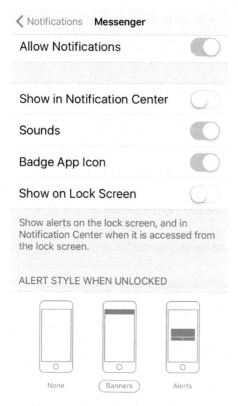

Figure 3-2. *Use an app's notification settings to control how often and where you see its notifications*

You now have the following choices for configuring the app's notifications:

- To stop the app's notifications altogether, tap the Allow Notifications switch to Off.

- To not see the app's notification in the Notification Center, tap the Show in Notification Center switch to Off.

- To not hear the app's notification sounds, tap the Sounds switch to Off. For some apps, you turn off notification sounds by tapping Sounds to see a list of sounds, then tapping None.

- To not see the app's badge icon, tap the Badge App Icon switch to Off.

- To not see the app's notifications on the Lock screen, tap the Show on Lock Screen switch to Off.

- Use the Alert Style When Unlocked section to choose the style you prefer for the app's notifications. Tap None to turn off alerts, or tap the style you want: Banners (which disappear automatically after a few seconds) or Alerts (which don't disappear until you dismiss them).

Your Facebook Data Doesn't Appear in the Contacts or Calendar App

iOS comes with Facebook support built right in to the system. You can easily post links, photos, and other content to your Facebook Timeline, and even send simple status updates without having to load the Facebook app. However, this baked-in Facebook support is far less of a convenience if you can't see your Facebook friends in the Contacts app or your Facebook events in the Calendar app.

Solution: If you're not seeing your Facebook friends in the Contacts app, here are two things to try:

- In the Settings app, tap Facebook and then tap the Contacts switch to On.

- In the Contacts app, tap Groups and then tap to activate the All Facebook group.

If you're not seeing your Facebook events in the Calendar app, try the following:

- In the Settings app, tap Facebook and then tap the Calendar switch to On.

- In the Calendar app, tap Calendars and then tap to activate the Facebook Events calendar.

An App is Frozen

If your iOS device screen freezes, the cause could be an app that has crashed.

Solution: You can usually get your device back in the saddle by forcing the app to quit. There are two techniques you can try:

- Press and hold the Sleep/Wake button until you see the Slide to Power Off screen; then press and hold the Home button for about 6 seconds. iOS shuts down the app and returns you to the Home screen.

- If an app is frozen but your device still works fine otherwise, double-press the Home button to display the multitasking screen, scroll right or left as needed to bring the app's thumbnail screen into view, then drag the app thumbnail up to the top of the screen. Your iPhone sends the thumbnail off the screen and shuts down the app.

Your Screen Won't Respond to Taps

Every now and then, your iOS device might freeze and no amount of tapping, swiping, or threatening will get the phone to respond. The most likely problem is that the touchscreen has become temporarily stuck. To fix that, press the Sleep/Wake button to put the device to sleep, press Sleep/Wake again to wake the device, and then drag Slide to Unlock. In most cases, you should now be able to resume normal iOS operations.

If that doesn't work, then it's possible that the app you're using has crashed, so you need to shut it down as I described in the "An app is frozen" section.

An App Is Taking up a Large Amount of Space

Your iOS device is so useful and so much fun, it's easy to forget that it has limitations, especially when it comes to storage. This is particularly true if you have a 16GB device, but even a device with greater capacity can fill up in a hurry if you stuff it with movies, TV shows, and tons of magazine subscriptions.

You can tell how much free space your device has left either by connecting it to iTunes or by tapping Settings, then General, and then Storage & iCloud Usage. The Storage & iCloud Usage screen not only shows you how much storage space you have available but also lets you tap Manage Storage to see how much space each app is using.

If you see that your device is running low on space, check the apps to see if any of them are taking up more than their fair share of hard drive real estate.

Solution: If you see a hard drive hog, you have two ways to delete its data and give your device some room to breathe:

- **Third-party apps.** For an app you picked up via the App Store, tap the app, tap Delete App, and then tap Delete App when your iPhone asks you to confirm.

- **Built-in apps.** For an app that came with iOS (such as Music or Video), tap the app to display a list of the data it's storing on your device, and then tap Edit. This puts the list in Edit mode. To remove an item, tap the red Delete button to the left of the item, and then tap the Delete button that appears (see Figure 3-3).

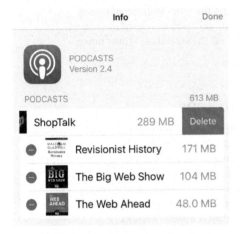

Figure 3-3. *To remove data from a built-in app, tap the red Delete button and then tap the Delete button that appears*

You Want to Control Third-Party Usage of Your Apps

Every so often an app will request access to another app on your device, such as Contacts, Calendars, or Photos. If you've installed a lot of apps, you might have lost track which of these third-party programs have access to your other apps.

Solution: You can allow or revoke third-party app permission to specific apps by following these steps:

1. Open the Settings app and then tap Privacy.

2. Tap the app for which you want to control access. iOS displays a list of apps that have requested access to the app, as shown in Figure 3-4.

3. Beside each app, tap the switch to Off to revoke access, or On to allow access.

Figure 3-4. *You can allow or revoke third-party access to your apps*

You're Having Trouble Using the Handoff Feature

You can use the Handoff feature to start a task on your iOS device and then continue that task using a nearby Mac. (Handoff works the other way, as well: You can start a task on your Mac and then continue the task on your iOS device.) You might find, however, that Handoff doesn't work and you can't continue a task.

Solution: First, make sure that your devices meet the following guidelines to use Handoff:

- Your Mac must be running OS X Yosemite or later, or any version of macOS.

- Your Mac must support Bluetooth 4.0. To check, click the Apple icon, click About This Mac, click System Report, click Bluetooth, then read the LMP Version. If it says 0x6, then your Mac supports Bluetooth 4.0.

■ **Tip**   If your Mac doesn't support Bluetooth 4.0, you might still be able to use Continuity if you install the third-party Continuity Activation Tool, available from `https://github.com/dokterdok/Continuity-Activation-Tool`.

- Your iOS device must be running iOS 8 or later.

- Both your Mac and your device must be signed in to the same iCloud account.

- Your iOS device must be within about 33 feet of your Mac.

If that all checks out, make sure your Mac is configured to accept Handoff connections:

1. Open System Preferences.

2. Click General.

3. Click to select the Allow Handoff between this Mac and your iCloud devices check box.

Finally, make sure iOS is configured to accept Handoff connections:

1. Open the Settings app.

2. Tap General.

3. Tap Handoff.

4. Tap the Handoff switch to On.

Advanced App Troubleshooting

As a general rule, you never have to worry about opening "too many" iOS apps, because the system takes care of managing your apps and the resources they consume. However, I've included the following "problem" to give you a more advanced look at how iOS handles app opening and closing.

You Have Too Many Apps Open

On a Mac or PC, having too many programs open can cause problems with system resources, particularly memory. However, even though iOS supports multitasking, it doesn't suffer from the same too-many-apps troubles that plague desktop machines.

To understand why, first know that, at its most basic, multitasking on iOS means that whenever you run an app and then switch to another app, your device keeps the first app available in the background. In most cases, the first app does nothing while it's in the background — it doesn't take any processor time away from your current app and it doesn't use battery power. This means that you're free to open as many apps as you like. However, if the first app is performing some task and you switch to another app, the first app continues to perform the task in the background.

To get a firm grip on how iOS multitasking works, you need to understand the four modes an app can have on iOS:

- **Running State.** The app is open and has the focus of the system.

- **Closed State.** This mode means the app is completely shut down. If you reboot your device (by turning it off and then back on), all your apps are then in the Closed State.

- **Suspended State.** If you launch an app, then press the Home button to return to the Home screen, usually iOS places the running app into the Suspended State. This means the app remains loaded into memory, but it's not running, it's not using up processor time, and it's not draining the battery. However, the app still maintains its current conditions, so that when you return to it, the app resumes where you left off.

- **Background State.** If you launch an app, start some process such as playing music, and then press the Home button to return to the Home screen, your iPhone puts the app into the Background State, which means it keeps the app's process running in the background. When you return to the app, either you see the process still running or it has been completed.

It's important to note that the vast majority of apps go into the Suspended State when you switch to another app. However, if you launch an app and your device doesn't have enough free memory available, iOS starts putting suspended apps into the Closed State to free up memory.

This built-in resource management is why having a lot of apps "open" in the multitasking screen (that is, the screen that appears when you double-tap the Home button; see Figure 3-5). Almost all of those apps are in the Closed State, so they're not affecting system performance in the least. (For this reason, you should really think of the multitasking screen as the "most recently used apps" screen.)

Figure 3-5. *The iPhone multitasking screen can be quite busy with "open" apps, but few of them are using any system resources*

CHAPTER 4

■ ■ ■

Resolving Web Issues

We live in a world where the promise of "information at your fingertips" (IAYF, to those in the know) has gone from a pie-in-the-sky daydream just 10 or 15 years ago to let-me-look-that-up-for-you reality now. That's because our fingertips are never far from a device – particularly an iPhone or cellular-enabled iPad – that's connected to the Internet and its vast supply of information. Whether you need to resolve an argument, get directions to the nearest café, or remember the name of the actress who starred in *Blossom*, your iOS device is right there to help.

It helps that the Safari app that comes with iOS is a solid web browser that has all the features you're likely to need. It's a great browser, but unfortunately it's not a perfect one, so you might encounter frustrations both small and large that can get in the way of your web surfing. This chapter tackles many of the most common Safari irritations and annoyances and shows you how to either work around them or fix them once and for all. So the next time you're at a dinner party and someone claims that Dustin Hoffman was in *Star Wars*, you'll be able to set the record straight in record time.

Troubleshooting Web Surfing Problems

You Have Trouble Viewing the Page Text or Other Information

We're quite a number of years into the mobile web revolution, so it's surprising how many websites are still not optimized for mobile viewing. This means you'll often visit a site that was built with a desktop browser in mind, so the text, images and other data appear unreadably tiny, especially on a smaller iPhone or iPod touch screen.

Solution: Many websites enable you to zoom in on the page by placing two fingers on the screen and spreading them apart. A quick way to zoom in on a page that has various sections is to double-tap on the specific section – it could be an image, a paragraph, a table, or a column of text – that you want magnified. Safari zooms the section to fill the width of the screen. Double-tap again to return the page to the regular view.

© Paul McFedries 2017
P. McFedries, *Troubleshooting iOS*, DOI 10.1007/978-1-4842-2445-8_4

■ **Note** The double-tap-to-zoom trick doesn't work on all pages. If the web page developer has set the page's maximum-scale property to 1, it means you can't zoom the page to anything larger than its original size.

It Takes a Long Time to Scroll Back to the Top of a Long Web Page

Although most web pages contain only a screenful or two of text and images, some pages are quite lengthy and consist of many screens. If you're reading a particularly long-winded web page and you're near the bottom, you may have quite a long way to scroll if you need to head back to the top to get to the address/search bar.

Solution: Save the wear and tear on your flicking finger! Instead, tap the status bar at the top of the screen once to display the address/search bar, then tap the status bar a second time; Safari immediately transports you to the top of the page.

■ **Tip** If you're using any model of the iPhone 6 or later, you might find it hard to reach the top of the screen if you're surfing one-handed. Remember that you can lightly double-tap the Home button to drop the Safari screen down halfway and bring its top bar within easy reach.

You Want to View a Website's Desktop Version

Many websites recognize that you're surfing with an iOS device and display a "mobile" version of the site. This version is usually easier to read and navigate, but that ease almost always comes at the cost of having access to fewer site features.

Solution: If a site isn't displaying the feature you want, you can request the site's "desktop" version (that is, the full version that you'd see if you were using a desktop browser). Follow these steps:

1. Swipe down on the screen to reveal the menu bar.

2. Tap the Share button.

3. In the bottom list of share actions, tap Request Desktop Site, as shown in Figure 4-1.

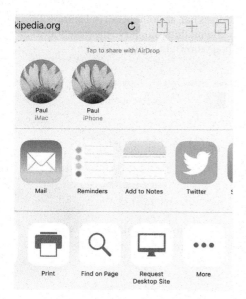

Figure 4-1. *To switch a site from mobile to desktop, tap Share, then tap Request Desktop Site*

You Find a Web Page's Extra Features Too Distracting

Reading an article or essay online is no picnic. The problem is the sheer amount of distraction on almost any page: background colors or images that clash with the text; ads above, to the side of, and within the text; site features such as search boxes, feed links, and content lists; and those ubiquitous icons for sharing the article with your friends on Facebook, Twitter, Pinterest, and on and on. Even worse, many of these features blink or change, so reading the page content is a real challenge.

Solution: Safari can help you solve this problem by offering the Reader feature for pages that support it. Reader removes all those extraneous page distractions that just get in the way of your reading pleasure. So, instead of a cacophony of text, icons, and images, you see pure, simple, large-enough-to-be-easily-read text. How do you arrive at this blissful state? By tapping the title bar at the top of the Safari screen and then tapping the Reader button, which appears on the left side of the address bar, as pointed out in Figure 4-2. Safari instantly transforms the page, and you see something similar to the page shown in Figure 4-3 (which is the Reader version of the page shown in Figure 4-2).

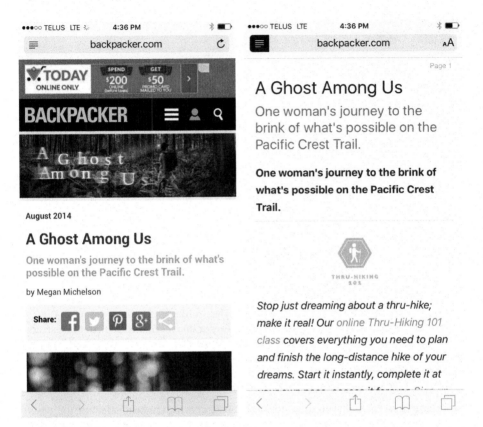

Figure 4-2. Today's web pages are all too often festooned with ads, icons, and other bric-a-brac

Figure 4-3. The Reader version of a web page is a simple and easy-to-read text affair

You Want to Open New Tabs in the Background

Depending on your iOS device and your version of iOS, when you tap and hold a link and then tap Open in New Tab, you might find that Safari immediately switches to the new tab and loads the link while you wait. That's often the behavior you want because it lets you view the new web page as soon as it loads. However, you might find that most of the time you prefer to stay on the current web page and check out the new tab later.

Solution: Having to perform the extra tap to get back to the current tab gets old in a hurry. The solution is to configure Safari to always open new tabs in the background. (This setting is off by default on the iPhone and iPod touch, but on by default on the iPad.) Follow these steps:

1. On the Home screen, tap Settings. The Settings app slides in.

2. Tap Safari. iOS displays the Safari screen.

3. On the iPhone or iPod touch, tap Open Links and then tap In Background, as shown in Figure 4-4. On the iPad, tap the Open New Tabs in Background switch to On.

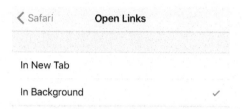

Figure 4-4. *On the iPhone or iPod touch, tap In Background in the Open Links screen*

You Want to Read One or More Pages While You're Offline

In your web travels, you'll often come upon a page with fascinating content that you can't wait to read. Unfortunately, a quick look at the length of the article tells you that you're going to need more time than you currently have available. You have a long flight or other stretch of offline time coming up, so that would be perfect, but how do you save web content for offline reading?

Solution: You can take advantage of a Safari feature called the Reading List. As the name implies, this is a simple list of things to read. When you don't have time to read something now, add it to your Reading List and you can read it at your leisure, even when you're not connected to the Internet.

There are a couple of techniques you can use to add a page to your Reading List:

- Use Safari to navigate to the page that you want to read later, tap the Share button, and then tap Add to Reading List.

- Tap and hold a link for the page that you want to read later and then tap Add to Reading List.

When you're ready to read, open Safari, tap the Bookmarks button, and then tap the Reading List tab, shown in Figure 4-5. Safari displays all the items you've added to the list and you just tap the article you want to read. To make the list a bit easier to manage, tap Show Unread to see just the pages you haven't yet perused.

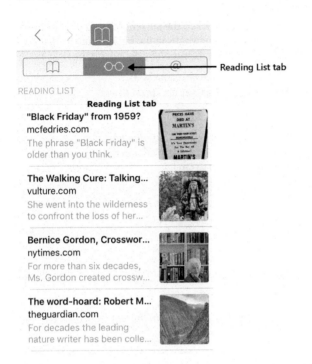

Figure 4-5. *Safari's Reading List tab contains the web pages you've saved for later*

Safari Does Not Offer to Save Website Passwords

A quintessential modern skill is remembering the dozens of usernames and passwords that give us entry into our favorite websites. Safari can help here by offering to store a website's account data and then enter it automatically each subsequent time. That's a major timesaver, but sometimes Safari doesn't offer to save a site's login data.

Solution: There are three main reasons why Safari might not be offering to save a site's username and password:

- Some websites request that browsers not save passwords, and Safari honors those requests. In this case, you can add the password manually, as shown below.

- Safari might be configured to not save usernames and passwords. To check, open Settings, tap Safari, tap AutoFill, and then tap the Names and Passwords switch to On.

- Safari might be in Private Browsing mode, in which case it does not save *any* data, including website login data. To check, open Safari and examine the menu bar. If the menu bar appears black or dark gray (see Figure 4-6) instead of white or light gray, then Safari is in Private Browsing mode. To fix this, exit Private Browsing mode by tapping the Tabs icon and then tapping the Private button to deactivate it.

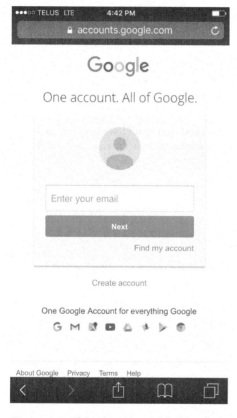

Figure 4-6. *If the menu bar is black or dark gray, Safari is in Private Browsing mode and it won't offer to save website username or passwords*

Here are the steps to follow to enter a website's username and password manually:

1. Tap Settings to display the Settings app.

2. Tap Safari. The Safari screen appears.

3. Tap Passwords. Settings prompts you for your passcode or Touch ID.

4. Enter your passcode or Touch ID. The Passwords screen appears.

5. Tap Add Password. The Add Password screen appears.

6. Fill in the website's address, your username, and your password. The password appears in regular text instead of the usual dots, so make sure no one's peeking over your shoulder as you do this.

7. Tap Done. iOS saves the login data for the site.

You Want to Save Your Credit Card Data

Shopping is a favorite online pastime, and it's one where, if you do it often enough, entering your credit card's number and expiration data by hand get can tiresome.

Solution: You can save your credit card data in Safari so you don't have to constantly enter your card's particulars. Follow these steps to configure Safari to save your credit card data when you make online purchases:

1. In the Home screen, tap Settings to open the Settings app.

2. Tap Safari. The Safari screen appears.

3. Tap AutoFill to open the AutoFill screen.

4. Tap the Credit Cards switch to On.

■ **Tip** Instead of adding your credit card data by hand, Safari enables you to enter the data automatically using the camera. In the AutoFill screen, tap Saved Credit Cards, enter your passcode (you really should use a passcode or Touch ID if you're adding credit cards to your iOS device; see Chapter 9), then tap Add Credit Card. Tap Use Camera, position the credit card within the camera field, and then wait until the card info is recognized.

You Want to View a Site's Pop-up Window

Pop-up ads have been a scourge on the web for almost as long as there has been a web. The frustration caused by these irritants was so great that, for a while now, all modern browsers have included a pop-up blocker that is activated by default, and iOS Safari is no exception.

However, not all pop-up windows are annoyances. Some might show useful information or a key feature of a website's interface. With pop-ups blocked, however, you miss out on this information or feature.

Solution: You can temporarily turn off Safari's pop-up blocker when you visit a site that has a pop-up window you want to see. Here are the steps to follow:

1. In the Home screen, tap Settings to display the Settings app.

2. Tap Safari. The Safari screen appears.

3. Tap the Block Pop-ups switch to Off, as shown in Figure 4-7.

Figure 4-7. *To temporarily allow a site's pop-up windows, tap the Block Pop-ups switch to Off, then visit the site*

You can now use Safari to visit the site, and its pop-up window will appear in a new tab. When you're done with that site, follow the above steps once again to tap the Block Pop-ups switch back to On.

You Want to View a Link's Address Before Tapping It

As you know, in iOS Safari you "click" a link in a web page by tapping it. These days, however, a savvy surfer always checks a link's address before clicking it because you just never know where you might end up. The address doesn't always indicate a nefarious or shady site, but it doesn't hurt to check.

In a regular web browser, you can see where a link takes you (that is, you can see the link's URL) by hovering the mouse pointer over the link and checking out the link address in the status bar. That doesn't work in iOS Safari, so how can you find out the address of a link before tapping it?

Solution: Tap and hold the link for a few seconds. Safari then displays a pop-up screen showing the link text and, more importantly, the URL, as shown in Figure 4-8. If the link looks legit, either tap Open to surf there in the current browser page or tap Open in New Page to start a fresh page. If you decide not to follow the link, tap outside the menu.

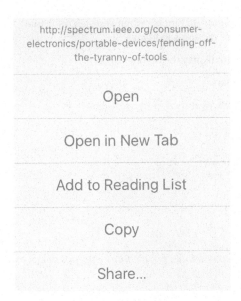

Figure 4-8. *Tap and hold a link to check its address for surfing to the site*

Troubleshooting Searching Problems
You Want to Use a Different Search Engine

Google is the default search engine on iOS. Almost everyone uses Google, of course, but if you have something against it, you might want to switch and use a different search engine. For example, many people dislike Google's add-tracking, so they switch to DuckDuckGo, which doesn't track its users.

Solution: You can use Safari to navigate to another search engine's URL and search from there. However, Safari's default search engine is more convenient because it means you can search directly from the address box. Although Google is the default search engine for iOS, it's not the only one it supports. Here are the steps to follow to set up a different search engine as the Safari default:

1. Open the Settings app.

2. Tap Safari. The Safari screen appears.

3. Tap Search Engine. iOS opens the Search Engine screen.

4. Tap the search engine you want to use. As shown in Figure 4-9, you have four choices: Google, Yahoo, Bing, or DuckDuckGo.

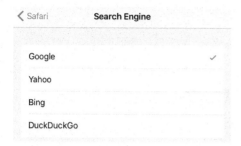

Figure 4-9. *In the Search Engine screen, tap the search engine you want to use as the default in Safari*

It Is Difficult to Find Specific Information within a Web Page

When you're perusing a page on the web, it's not unusual to be looking for specific information. In those situations, rather than reading through the entire page to find the info you seek, it would be a lot easier to search for the data. You can easily do this in the desktop version of Safari or any other computer browser, but, at first glance, the Safari app doesn't seem to have a "Find" feature anywhere.

Solution: Safari *does* offer such a feature, but you need to know where to look:

1. Use the Safari app to navigate to the web page that contains the information you seek.

2. Tap the web page title bar (or swipe down on the screen) to display the menu bar, and then tap inside the address/search box at the top of the Safari window.

3. Type the search text you want to use. Safari displays the web page matches, but at the bottom of those matches it also displays "On This Page (X matches)," where X is the number of times your search text appears on the web page.

4. Flick the search results up to hide the keyboard.

5. Tap Find "search" (where search is the search text you entered). Safari highlights the first instance of the search term. The On This Page message now appears at the bottom of the results screen, as shown in Figure 4-10.

Fending Off The Tyranny of Tools

"Distracting Ourselves to Death" isn't just a metaphor anymore

By Paul McFedries
Posted 28 Jul 2016 | 15:00 GMT

If you program, you will occasionally need some useful bit of code from an online source such as Stack Overflow. You might then have noticed something interesting: If you simply copy and paste the code, you don't remember it and often have to repeat the process later on. However, if you *type* the code yourself, then you are much more likely to remember it.

∧ ∨ 1 of 7 matches   🔍 tool   **Done**

Figure 4-10. *The On This Page message tells you the number of matches that appear on the current web page*

6. Tap the down-pointing arrow to cycle forward through the instances of the search term that appear on the page. Note that you can also cycle backward through the results by tapping the up-pointing arrow. Also, when you tap the down-pointing arrow after the last result appears, Safari returns you to the first result.

7. When you're finished with the search, tap Done.

You Want to Search the Web Using Voice Commands

You can use Safari to type search queries either directly into the search box or by navigating to a search engine site. However, these days typing suddenly seems like such a quaint pastime thanks to the voice-recognition prowess of the Siri app. So why type a search query when you can just tell Siri what you're looking for?

Solution: Launch Siri by pressing and holding the Home button (or pressing and holding the Mic button of the device headphones, or the equivalent button on a Bluetooth headset). Here are some general tips for web searching with Siri:

- **Searching the entire web.** Say "Search the web for *topic*," where *topic* is your search criteria.

- **Searching Wikipedia.** Say "Search Wikipedia for *topic*," where *topic* is the subject you want to look up.

- **Searching with a particular search engine.** Say "*Engine topic*," where *Engine* is the name of the search engine, such as Google or Bing (although not DuckDuckGo, for some reason), and *topic* is your search criteria.

Siri also understands commands related to searching for businesses and restaurants through its partnership with Yelp. To look for businesses and restaurants using Siri, the general syntax to use is the following (although, as usual with Siri, you don't have to be too rigid about this):

"Find (or Look for) *something somewhere.*"

Here, the *something* part can be the name of a business (such as "Starbucks"), a type of business (such as "gas station"), a type of restaurant (such as "Thai restaurants"), or a generic product (such as "coffee"). The *somewhere* part can be something relative to your current location (such as "around here" or "near me" or "within walking distance") or a specific location (such as "in Indianapolis" or "in Broad Ripple"). Here are some examples:

- "Find a gas station within walking distance."

- "Look for pizza restaurants in Indianapolis."

- "Find coffee around here."

- "Look for a grocery store near me."

Note, too, that if you add a qualifier such as "good" or "best" before the *something* portion of the command, Siri returns the results organized by their Yelp ratings.

CHAPTER 5

■ ■ ■

Overcoming Email Glitches

These days, we have an impressive number of ways to communicate with each other: texting, SnapChatting, video calling, Facebook messaging, Twitter direct messaging, and so many more. These newfangled (more or less) communications technologies get all the press and all the glory, not surprisingly. But when it comes to day-to-day, bread-and-butter communications, most of us fall back on good old email. It's not sexy, it hasn't changed all that much in a couple of decades, and whatever bells and whistles a developer adds to an email client are usually ignored. Email just gets the job done.

Or, I should say, email *usually* gets the job done. Like any technology, email suffers from its share of glitches and bugs, so you might find that you have trouble sending or receiving email messages using the iOS Mail app. The good news is that most of these problems are readily fixable and you get usually get Mail back on its feet in short order. To help you do that, this chapter offers a collection of the most common email complaints, as well as their solutions.

Troubleshooting Sending Email
Mail Uses the Wrong Account When Sending

When you add more than one email account, how does Mail decide which of those to use when you send a new message? It designates one of those accounts – specifically, the first account you added to the Mail app – as the default, and it then automatically uses that address as the sending account each time you compose a new message. It also uses that address as the default sending account when you when you share content such as a link, photo, or map via email.

■ **Note**   Mail does not use the default account automatically when you reply to or forward a message. In those cases, Mail configures the reply or forward to be sent from the account to which the original message was addressed.

© Paul McFedries 2017
P. McFedries, *Troubleshooting iOS*, DOI 10.1007/978-1-4842-2445-8_5

If the default account is the one you want to use to send a message, then this behavior isn't a problem, but you might prefer to use one of your other accounts.

Solution: First, note that you're not restricted to using the default account for every message. If you need to use a different account when sending a message, follow these steps:

1. In the Mail app, start a new message.

2. Tap the Cc/Bcc, From line in the New Message screen.

3. Tap the From line. Mail displays a list of the available email addresses, as shown in Figure 5-1.

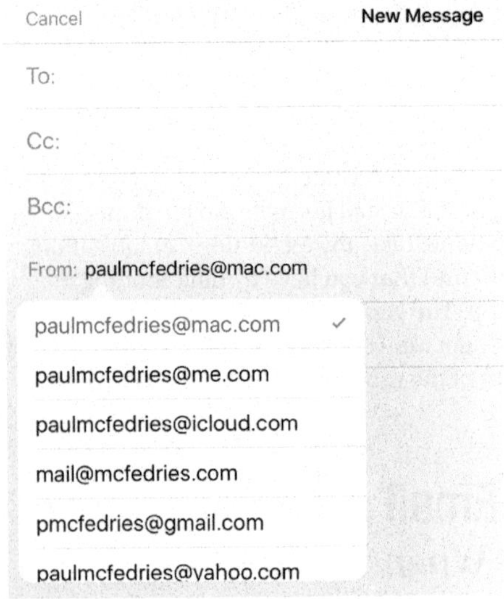

Cancel   **New Message**

To:

Cc:

Bcc:

From: paulmcfedries@mac.com

paulmcfedries@mac.com   ✓

paulmcfedries@me.com

paulmcfedries@icloud.com

mail@mcfedries.com

pmcfedries@gmail.com

paulmcfedries@yahoo.com

Figure 5-1. You can use the From list to select a different sending address

4. Tap the address you want to use to send the message.

Changing the sending account as needed works well if you only have to use that technique occasionally, but it's not something you'll want to run through each time you send a message. If there's a particular account that you prefer to use for sending all or most of the time, then you need to set up that account as the default. Here are the steps to follow:

1. On the Home screen, tap Settings. The Settings app appears.

2. Tap Mail to open the Mail screen. iOS displays the Mail screen.

3. Near the bottom of the Mail section, tap Default Account. This opens the Default Account screen, which displays a list of your accounts. The current default account is shown with a check mark beside it.

4. Tap the account you want to use as the default. iOS places a check mark beside the account, as shown in Figure 5-2.

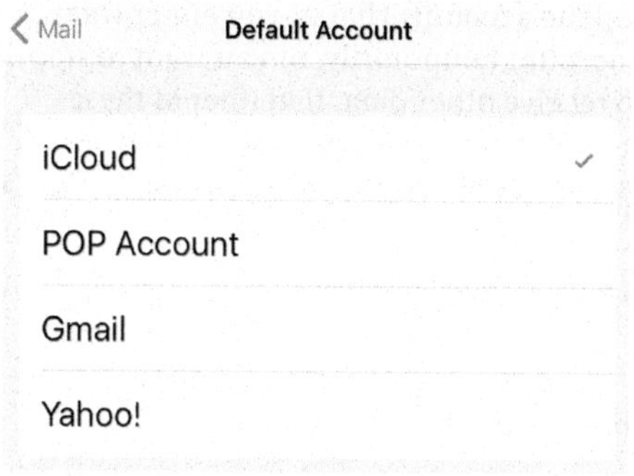

❮ Mail   **Default Account**

iCloud   ✓

POP Account

Gmail

Yahoo!

Figure 5-2. *In the Default Account screen, tap the account you want Mail to use as the default for sending messages*

You Want to Prevent an Account from Receiving Email

There are many reasons why you might want Mail to prevent a particular account from receiving email temporarily:

- The Mail app checks for new messages at a regular interval, so if you have several accounts configured in Mail, this incessant checking can put quite a strain on your device battery. By preventing one or more accounts from receiving messages, you reduce that strain.

- An account might receive a large number of messages in a short time. Rather than wasting time and resources receiving all those messages on your device, you might prefer to prevent them from being received in iOS and then handle them in your regular email client.

- An account might receive one or more very large messages. Rather than subjecting your device to these behemoths, you might want to prevent them from being downloaded so you can process the messages more easily using your desktop or web email client.

Alternatively, you might want to *never* receive email on a particular account, but you still might want to work with that account's other data, such as its calendars or contacts.

■ **Note**   Turning off email while still retaining other types of data such as calendars and contacts only works for the following account types: iCloud, Exchange, Google, Yahoo!, AOL, and Outlook.com. You can't do this with POP (Post Office Protocol) or IMAP (Internet Message Access Protocol) accounts.

Solution: First, I assume you still want to keep the account. That is, you either want to stop receiving messages on a particularly account temporarily, or you want to stop receiving email permanently but still want to receive other data. If neither of these is the case, then you probably want to delete the account, as described in the next section. Otherwise, you want to disable the account's email receiving capability. Here's how you do it:

1. On the Home screen, tap Settings to open the Settings app.

2. Tap Mail to open the Mail screen.

3. Tap the account you want to disable. iOS displays the account's settings.

4. Depending on the type of account, use one of the following techniques to temporarily disable the account:

   - For an iCloud, Exchange, Google, Yahoo!, AOL, or Outlook.com account, tap the Mail switch to Off, as shown in Figure 5-3.

   - For a POP or IMAP account, tap the Account switch to Off.

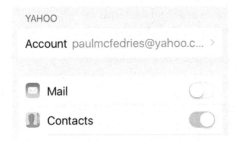

Figure 5-3. *For an iCloud, Exchange, Google, Yahoo!, AOL, or Outlook.com account, tap the Mail switch to Off*

When you're ready to work with the account again, repeat these steps to tap the Mail switch or the Account switch back to On.

You No Longer Need an Account

An email account you no longer use is cluttering your Mail Inbox, taking up storage space, and wasting battery power with constant checks for new messages.

Solution: If don't use an email account any longer, you should delete it. This will remove the account and its messages from Mail, free up some storage space, speed up sync times, and save battery power.

■ **Note** If you find that you can't send email using a particular account, even after trying the troubleshooting steps found throughout this chapter, then one technique that often works is to delete the account and then add it back again.

Follow these steps to delete an account:

1. Open the Settings app.

2. Tap Mail to open the Mail screen.

3. Tap the account you want to delete. This opens the account's settings.

4. At the bottom of the screen, tap Delete Account. iOS asks you to confirm.

5. Tap Delete, as shown in Figure 5-4. iOS removes the account.

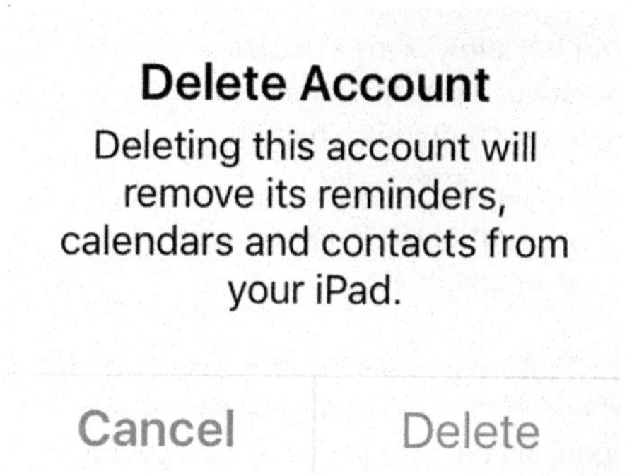

Delete Account

Deleting this account will remove its reminders, calendars and contacts from your iPad.

Cancel   Delete

Figure 5-4. Tap the account and then tap Delete Account to remove it from Mail

You Want to Save an Unfinished Email Message

If you're composing a message on your computer and decide to work on it later, your mail program stores the message as a draft that you can reopen any time. The Mail app doesn't appear to have that option, so how can you save an unfinished message?

Solution: The Mail app doesn't *appear* to offer the option of saving a draft of a message, but it does, albeit in a very unintuitive way. In the message window, tap Cancel and then tap Save Draft (see Figure 5-5). When you're ready to resume editing, open the account in the Mailboxes screen, tap Drafts, and then tap your saved message.

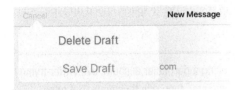

Figure 5-5. *To save an unfinished message, tap Cancel and then tap Save Draft*

Troubleshooting Outgoing Email Problems When Using a Third-Party Account

For security reasons, some Internet service providers (ISPs) insist that all their customers' outgoing mail must be routed through the ISP's SMTP (Simple Mail Transport Protocol) server. This usually isn't a big deal if you're using an email account maintained by the ISP, but it can lead to the following problems if you are using an account provided by a third party (such as your website host):

- Your ISP might block messages sent using the third-party account because it thinks you're trying to relay the message through the ISP's server (a technique often used by spammers).

- You might incur extra charges if your ISP allows only a certain amount of SMTP bandwidth per month or a certain number of sent messages, whereas the third-party account offers higher limits or no restrictions at all.

- You might have performance problems, with the ISP taking much longer to route messages than the third-party host.

Solution: To work around these problems, many third-party hosts offer access to their SMTP server via a port other than the standard port 25. For example, the iCloud SMTP server (smtp.icloud.com) also accepts connections on ports 465 and 587. Ask your mail hosting provider which port (or ports) they support.

Here's how to configure an email account to use a nonstandard SMTP port:

1. On the Home screen, tap Settings. You see the Settings app.

2. Tap Mail. The Mail settings screen appears.

3. Tap the POP account you want to configure. The account's settings screen appears.

4. Near the bottom of the screen, tap SMTP. iOS displays the SMTP screen.

5. In the Primary Server section, tap the server. iOS displays the server settings.

6. In the Outgoing Mail Server section, tap Server Port and then type the port number.

7. Tap Done.

■ **Note** You might also find you have trouble sending email over a cellular connection. To learn how to troubleshoot that problem, see Chapter 2's "You Can send Email Over Wi-Fi But Not Over Cellular" section.

Mail Cannot Send POP Messages Using a Particular Account

When you send a POP message using Mail, you might find that the message either stays in the Outbox folder (meaning it never gets sent) or is never delivered (in which case, you might or might not receive a bounce message). There are many reasons why a message doesn't get sent, but it usually boils down to one or more of the following misconfigured POP account settings.

- Using an incorrect SMTP host name.

- Using an incorrect user name or password.

- Not using SSL (Secure Sockets Layer) encryption if your email host requires it (or, conversely, using SLL when your host does not require it).

- Not using authentication. To reduce spam, many ISPs now require SMTP authentication for outgoing mail, which means that you must log on to the SMTP server to confirm that you're the person sending the mail (as opposed to some spammer spoofing your address). If your ISP requires authentication on outgoing messages, you need to configure your email account to provide the proper credentials.

- Using a server port that is not supported by the email host.

If you're not too sure about any of this, check with your email host.

Solution: Follow these steps to configure your email account with the correct settings:

1. On the Home screen, tap Settings. iOS displays the Settings app.

2. Tap Mail. The Mail settings screen appears.

3. Tap the POP account you want to configure. The account's settings screen appears.

4. Near the bottom of the screen, tap SMTP. iOS displays the SMTP screen.

5. In the Primary Server section, tap the server. iOS displays the server's settings screen.

6. Check the values in the Host Name and User Name fields to ensure they're correct.

7. Retype the correct password.

8. Tap the SSL switch to On if your host requires SSL; otherwise, tap this switch to Off.

9. Tap Authentication to open the Authentication screen, tap the type of authentication required by your host (usually Password), and then tap Back to return to the server settings screen.

10. Check that the Server Port setting is a port value supported by your host.

11. Tap Done.

You're Having Trouble Sending Email Using Siri Voice Commands

You can use the Siri voice recognition app to check, compose, send, and reply to messages, all with simple voice commands. Tap and hold the Home button (or press and hold the Mic button of the device headphones, or the equivalent button on a Bluetooth headset) until Siri appears. Siri is handy, but you might have trouble getting it to do what you want.

Solution: Make sure you're using commands that Siri recognizes.

To check for new email messages on your iCloud account, you need only say "Check email" (or just "Check mail"). You can also view a list of iCloud messages as follows:

- To display unread messages, say "Show new email."

- To display messages from a particular person, say "Show email from *name*," where *name* is the name of the sender.

To start a new email message, Siri gives you several options:

- To create a new message addressed to a particular person, say "Email *name*," where *name* is the name of the recipient. This name can be a name from your Contacts list or someone with a defined relationship, such as "Mom" or "my brother."

- To create a new message with a particular subject line, say "Email *name* about *subject*," where *name* defines the recipient, and *subject* is the subject line text.

- To create a new message and also specify the body text, say "Email *name* about *subject* and say *text*," where *name* is the recipient, *subject* is the subject line, and *text* is the message body text.

In each case, Siri creates the new message, displays it, and then asks if you want to send it. If you do, you can either say "Send" or tap the Send button.

If you have a message displayed, you can send back a response by saying "Reply." If you want to add some text to the response, say "Reply *text*," where *text* is your response.

You can also use Siri within Mail to dictate a message. When you tap inside the body of a new message, the keyboard that appears shows a Mic icon beside the spacebar. Tap the Mic icon and then start dictating. Here are some notes:

- For punctuation, you can say the name of the mark you need, such as "comma" (,), "semicolon" (;), "colon" (:), "period" or "full stop" (.), "question mark" (?), "exclamation point" (!), "dash" (-), or "at sign" (@).

- You can enclose text in parentheses by saying "open parenthesis," then the text, and then "close parenthesis."

- To surround text with quotation marks, say "open quote," then the text, then "close quote."

- To render a word in all uppercase letters, say "all caps" and then say the word.

- To start a new paragraph, say "new line."

- You can have some fun by saying "smiley face" for :-), "wink face" for ;-), and "frown face" for :-(.

When you're finished, tap Done.

Troubleshooting Receiving Email

You Receive Email on Your Device, but Not on Your Computer

If you need to check email on multiple devices, you first need to understand how POP email messages are delivered over the Internet. (This does not apply to iCloud, Gmail, and other services that use IMAP.) When someone sends you a message, it doesn't come directly to your iOS device or computer. Instead, it goes to the server that your Internet service provider (or your company) has set up to handle incoming messages. When you ask Mail to check for new messages, it communicates with the POP server to see if any messages are waiting in your account. If so, Mail downloads those messages and then instructs the server to delete the copies of the messages stored on the server. So if you retrieve messages on your iOS device, they will no longer by available to download to your computer.

Solution: You need to configure Mail so that it leaves a copy of the messages on the POP server after you download them. That way, the messages are still available when you check messages using another device. Note that this is the default behavior for POP accounts that you add to iOS. Therefore, if you find that you're receiving messages on your iOS device but not elsewhere, then you need to follow these steps to prevent iOS from deleting messages from the server:

1. On the Home screen, tap Settings.

2. Tap Mail to open the Mail screen to display the Mail screen.

3. Tap the POP account you want to configure. The account's settings screen appears.

4. Near the bottom of the screen, tap Advanced. iOS displays the Advanced screen.

5. Tap Delete from server. The Delete from server screen appears.

6. Tap Never, as shown in Figure 5-6.

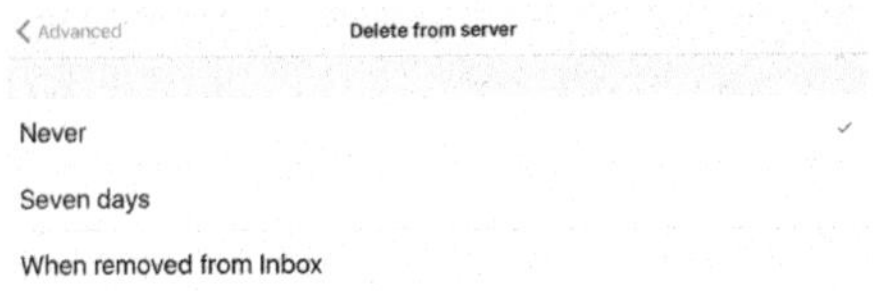

Figure 5-6. *To ensure that Mail leaves a copy of downloaded messages on the POP server, tap Never in the Delete from server screen*

You Receive a Great Deal of Spam

It's sad to say that there are no longer any spam-free zones. If you have an Internet-based email account, you get spam. End of story. In fact, you most likely don't get only one or two spams a day, but more like one or two dozen. That's not surprising because spam now accounts for the majority of the billions of messages sent every day, and on some days it even accounts for 90 percent of all sent messages! ISPs and email hosting companies are getting better at filtering out spam before it gets to you, but these defenses remain sadly incomplete.

Solution: It's no longer possible to avoid spam, but there are some things you can do to minimize how much of it you have to wade through each day:

- Never type your actual email address in a forum or blog post comment. The most common method that spammers use to gather addresses is to harvest them from online posts. One common tactic you can use is to alter your email address by adding text that invalidates the address, but is still obvious for other people to figure out. Here's an example: yourname@ yourisp.remove-this-to-email-me.com.

- Consider creating an email address to use exclusively for logins, mailing lists, newsletters, and other online uses. That address will likely attract spam eventually, but it's better than compromising your main email address.

- If you see a message in your Inbox that you're sure is spam, don't tap it. Doing so can sometimes notify the spammer that you've opened the message, which confirms that your address is legitimate. You can prevent this by disabling remote images, as described in the next section.

■ **Tip** If you see a definite spam message in your Inbox, you can delete it without tapping it. Either perform a short swipe left on the message and then tap Trash, or perform a long swipe left on the message until it disappears from the Inbox.

- Never respond to spam. Don't respond, even to an address within the spam that claims to be a "removal" address. By responding to the spam, you prove that your address is legitimate, so you just end up getting more spam.

- If you have an email address that gets a ton of spam, consider declaring "spam bankruptcy" and deleting the account, not only from your iOS device, but also from your ISP or mail host.

You Want to Disable Remote Images in Messages

A *web bug* is an image that resides on a remote server and is added to a HTML-formatted email message by referencing an address on the remote server. When you open the message, Mail uses the address to download the image for display within the message. That sounds harmless enough, but if the message is junk email, it's likely that the address also contains either your email address or a code that points to your email address. So when the remote server gets a request to load the image, it knows not only that you've opened the message but also that your email address is legitimate. So, not surprisingly, spammers use web bugs all the time because, for them, valid email addresses are a form of gold.

Solution: The iOS Mail app displays remote images by default. To disable remote images, follow these steps:

1.   On the Home screen, tap Settings. iOS opens the Settings app.

2.   Tap Mail to open the Mail settings screen.

3.   Tap the Load Remote Images switch to Off, as shown in Figure 5-7. Mail saves the setting and no longer displays remote images – particularly web bugs – in your email messages.

■ **Tip**   To display remote images in a non-spam message, tap the message and then tap Load All Images.

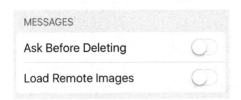

Figure 5-7.   To squash web bugs, tap the Load Remote Images switch to Off

You No Longer Want Mail to Organize Your Messages by Thread

In the Mail app, your messages get grouped by thread, which means the original message and all the replies you've received are grouped together in the account's Inbox folder.

Organizing messages by thread is usually convenient, but not always. For example, if your using an iPhone or iPod touch, sometimes you might view your messages and scroll through them by tapping the Next (right-pointing arrow) and Previous (left-pointing arrow) buttons. When you come to a thread, Mail jumps into the thread and you then scroll through each message in the thread, which can be a real hassle if the thread contains a large number of replies.

Solution: If you find that threads are more hassle than they're worth, you can follow these steps to configure Mail to no longer organize messages by thread:

1. On the Home screen, tap Settings. iOS opens the Settings app.

2. Tap Mail to open the Mail settings screen.

3. Tap the Organize By Thread switch to Off.

Deleted Messages Are Being Removed from the Trash Folder

When you delete a message, Mail doesn't remove the message completely, but only transfers it to the account's Trash folder. This is useful because if you delete a message by accident, you can recover the message by locating it in the Trash folder and moving it back to the Inbox (or its original folder). That is, you can recover the message *if* it still exists in the Trash folder. Unfortunately, Mail configures each account to automatically delete items from the Trash folder after one week.

Solution: Follow these steps to control when Mail deletes messages from the Trash folder:

1. On the Home screen, tap Settings to display the Settings app.

2. Tap Mail to display the Mail settings screen.

3. Tap the account you want to configure.

4. Display the account's advanced mail options:

    • For an iCloud account, tap Mail and then tap Advanced.

    • For a POP account, tap Advanced.

    • For most other account types, tap Account and then tap Advanced.

5. Tap Remove to open the Remove screen.

6. Tap Never to prevent Mail from removing messages automatically from the account's Trash folder, as shown in Figure 5-8.

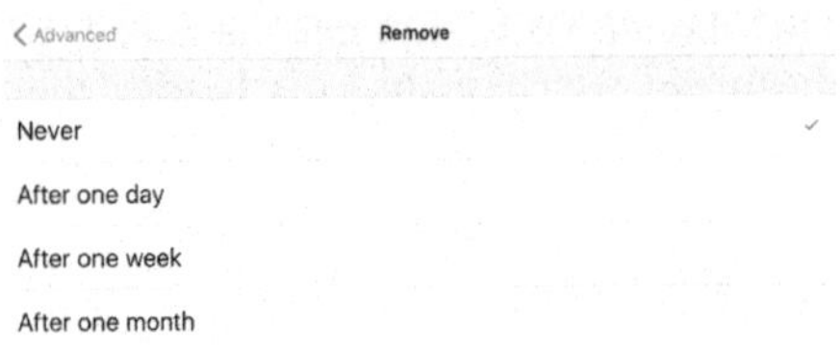

Never ✓

After one day

After one week

After one month

Figure 5-8. *In the Remove screen, tap Never to prevent Mail from automatically deleting messages from the account's Trash folder*

You Do Not See the All Inboxes Folder

If you have multiple accounts set up in iOS, Mail includes a folder named All Inboxes that shows a combined list of all the messages you've received on your accounts. This folder sometimes disappears after upgrading iOS.

Solution: Follow these steps to restore the All Inboxes folder to the Mail interface:

1. In the Mail app, display the Mailboxes screen.

2. Tap Edit.

3. Tap the All Inboxes item to activate it, as shown in Figure 5-9.

4. Tap Done.

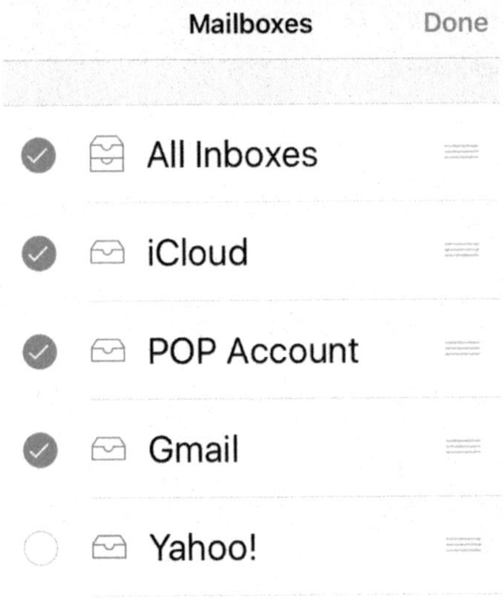

Mailboxes   Done

✓ 🗁 All Inboxes ☰

✓ 🖾 iCloud ☰

✓ 🖾 POP Account ☰

✓ 🖾 Gmail ☰

○ 🖾 Yahoo! ☰

Figure 5-9. *To restore the All Inboxes folder to the Mailboxes screen, tap Edit and then tap to activate the All Inboxes item*

CHAPTER 6

■ ■ ■

Fixing Phone Troubles

Most of the chapters in this book focus on the data-related features of iOS and its devices: Wi-Fi, apps, the Web, email, photos, and so on. That's apt because our iOS devices are computers, after all, so it makes sense to concentrate on troubleshooting computing tasks. But the iPhone is different. Sure, it makes an excellent mobile computer, but at its heart it's also a mobile phone. And while it's true that the phone call is beginning to feel more than a little like an anachronism, the "phone" part of this smartphone is still used by almost every iPhone owner, even those in their twenties. (A recent Pew Research poll found that 93 percent of smartphone owners aged 18 to 29 had used either voice or video calling.) The phone call's enduring appeal comes from a number of factors: it's immediate (assuming the other person picks up!), intimate, and efficient. But all this only applies if the iPhone's calling features are working properly and you know how to get the most out of them. This chapter looks at a few common calling concerns and shows you how to fix them or work around them.

Troubleshooting Incoming Calls

You Need to Silence an Incoming Call

When a call comes in, there might be times when you can't answer the phone right away. For example, if you're in a meeting, you might prefer to leave the room before answering the call to disturb the other meeting participants as little as possible. Of course, if the phone keeps ringing while you're making your way to the door, then you're still disturbing everyone.

Solution: As soon as you hear the incoming call, press the Sleep/Wake button once. This temporarily turns off the ringer, meaning that you still have the standard number of rings to answer, should you decide to. If you don't answer, your iPhone sends the call to your voicemail.

© Paul McFedries 2017
P. McFedries, *Troubleshooting iOS*, DOI 10.1007/978-1-4842-2445-8_6

You Can't Adjust the Volume of the Ringer Using the Volume Buttons

Rather than silencing an incoming call you might prefer just to turn the volume down a bit. However, when you press the Volume Down button on the side of the device, the ringer stays at the same volume.

Solution: If you can't turn the volume of the ringer up or down using the volume buttons, it means this feature has been disabled. To turn it back on, follow these steps:

1. Open the Settings app.

2. Tap Sounds.

3. Tap the Change with Buttons switch to On, as shown in Figure 6-1.

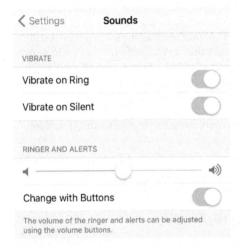

Figure 6-1. *Tap the Change with Buttons switch to On to control the ringer volume using the iPhone's volume buttons*

▦ **Caution**   On the other hand, locking the ringer volume is a good idea because it prevents one of the major iPhone frustrations: missing a call because the ringer volume has been muted accidentally (for example, by your iPhone getting jostled in a purse or pocket).

You Want to Send an Incoming Call Directly to Voicemail

You receive a phone call on your iPhone, but you can't answer it right now. However, you also don't want to disturb your neighbors by letting the phone ring until voicemail kicks in.

Solution: Use any of the following techniques:

- If the phone isn't locked, tap the red Decline button on the touchscreen.

- If you're using the EarPods, squeeze and hold the center button for two seconds.

- Press the Sleep/Wake button twice in quick succession.

Whichever method you use, iOS sends the call directly to voicemail. Note, however, that if you change your mind, you won't be able to answer the call.

You want to Be Able to Answer a Call Using Another Device

It has happened to all of us: you're in one room when you hear your iPhone ring in another room, and a mad dash ensues to try and answer the call before it goes to voicemail. It would be nice if that mad dash didn't have to take place and you could just answer the call using a handy iPad or Mac that's on the same Wi-Fi network as your iPhone.

Solution: iOS supports a feature that enables you to answer incoming calls on your other devices, including iPads, iPhones, and even Macs. To ensure this feature is activated and to control which devices you can use to answer calls, follow these steps:

1. Open the Settings app, and then tap Phone to display the Phone settings.

2. Tap Calls on Other Devices. If you don't see this setting, see the next problem.

3. Make sure the Allow Calls on Other Devices switch is set to On, as shown in Figure 6-2.

4. In the list of devices, tap the switch to On for each device that you want to use to answer calls.

Figure 6-2. Tap the Allow Calls on Other Devices switch to On, then tap the switch to On beside each device you want to use to answer calls

You Can't Access the Calls on Other Devices Setting

If you want to configure your iPhone to allow calls to appear on other iOS devices, you might find that the setting doesn't appear when you tap Phone in the Settings app.

Solution: You must be signed in to both iCloud and FaceTime using the same Apple ID before the Calls on Other Devices setting will appear. Follow these steps to sign in to these services:

1. Open the Settings app.

2. Tap iCloud.

3. If you are not already signed in to iCloud, type your Apple ID email address and password, then tap Sign In.

4. Tap Settings to return to the main Settings screen.

5. Tap FaceTime to open the FaceTime settings.

6. Tap the FaceTime switch to On.

7. If you are not signed in, tap Use your Apple ID for FaceTime, type your Apple ID email address and password, then tap Sign In.

You Want to Respond to a Call without Answering It

Earlier in this chapter you learned how to send an unwanted call directly to voicemail. That's great for calls you want to ignore, but there are plenty of situations where you can't answer the phone, but you also don't want to ignore the caller. For example, if you're expecting a call but get dragged into a meeting in the meantime, it would be rude to still answer the call when it comes in, but if you just send the call to voicemail your caller might wonder what's going on. Similarly, you might be a bit late for an appointment, and on your way there you see a call come in from the person you're meeting. Again, it might not be convenient to answer the call, but letting voicemail handle it might lead your caller to wonder if you're going to show up for the meeting.

Solution: iOS offers a feature that gives you an easy way to handle these sticky phone situations. It's called Respond with Text and it enables you to simultaneously decline a call and send the caller a prefab text message. That way, you avoid a voice conversation (which, depending on your current situation, might be rude or inconvenient), but you give the caller some feedback.

By default, Respond with Text comes with three ready-to-send messages:

> Sorry, I can't talk right now.
>
> I'm on my way.
>
> Can l call you later?

There's also an option to send a custom message if none of these is quite right. Here's how to decline an incoming call and send the caller a text message:

1. When the call comes in, tap Message, shown in Figure 6-3. Your iPhone displays a button for each of the prefab text messages.

▥ **Note**   You must have call display on your phone plan to see the Message button.

Figure 6-3. *Tap Message to reply to the caller with a text message*

2. Tap the reply you want to send. If you want to send a different message, tap Custom, type your message, and then tap Send.

The caller sees User Busy in the Phone app and then receives a text message.

■ **Note** If you're not all that fond of the default replies, you can forge your own. Tap Settings, tap Phone, tap Respond with Text, and then use the three text boxes to type your own messages.

You Want to Set a Reminder to Return a Phone Call

The Respond with Text feature is a handy trick to have up your iPhone sleeve, but it suffers from the same problem that plagues straight-up declining a call: if you want to talk to that person later, you have to remember to call back.

Solution: You *could* use the Reminders app to nudge yourself in an hour (or whenever) to make the return call. Fortunately, however, you don't need to perform that extra step because you can get the Phone app to do it for you. The Phone app has a feature that lets you decline a call and automatically create a callback reminder. You can set up the reminder to fire in one hour or when you leave your current location.

Here's how to decline an incoming call and set a callback reminder:

1. When the call comes in, tap Remind Me (see Figure 6-3, earlier). Your iPhone displays the callback reminder options shown in Figure 6-4.

Figure 6-4. When a call comes in, tap Remind Me to see the reminder options shown here

2.   Tap the type of reminder you want to set:

- **When I leave.** Tap this option to set a location-based reminder that triggers when you leave your current location.

- **In 1 hour.** Tap this option to set a time-based reminder.

■ **Tip**   If you don't see the When I leave reminder option, you need to turn on Location Services.

You Only Want to Allow Calls from Certain People

Rather than declining all incoming calls, you might be in a situation where you want to decline all calls *except* for those from a particular person or group.

Solution: You can do this by activating the Do Not Disturb feature and configuring it to allow calls from only the people you want to talk with.

This part of Do Not Disturb works with groups of people, not individuals. So your first task is to create or configure a group that consists of the people you want to allow to call you. You have two choices:

- In the Phone app, add each person to the Favorites list. Tap Contacts and then, for each person, tap the contact, tap Add to Favorites, and then tap Call. If the person has multiple numbers, tap the number you want to use as a favorite.

- Create a Contacts app group for the people you want to allow. Note, however, that the Contacts app doesn't offer a feature for creating groups. Instead, you need to sign into icloud.com, open Contacts, and then click the Add (+) button at the bottom of the Groups pane.

With your group set up, follow these steps to configure Do Not Disturb to allow calls only from the group:

1.   Tap Settings to open the Settings app.

2.   Tap Do Not Disturb. The Do Not Disturb screen appears.

3.   Tap the Manual switch to On to activate Do Not Disturb.

4. Tap Allow Calls From to open the Allow Calls From screen, shown in Figure 6-5.

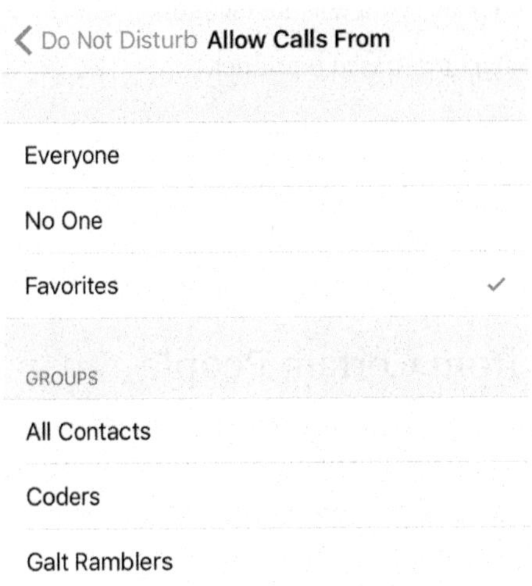

‹ Do Not Disturb **Allow Calls From**

Everyone

No One

Favorites   ✓

GROUPS

All Contacts

Coders

Galt Ramblers

Figure 6-5. *Use the Allow Calls From screen to choose the group that is allowed to call you while Do Not Disturb is activated*

5. Either tap Favorites or tap a contact group.

iOS will now allow a call through only if the caller is in the group you chose. When you want to accept all calls again, follow steps 1 to 3 to set the Manual switch to Off and deactivate Do Not Disturb. (Alternatively, if you want to keep the other Do Not Disturb features in place, follow steps 1 to 4 and then tap Everyone.)

You Don't Want to See Info about Other Calls While You're on a Call

If you're already on a call and another one comes in, your iPhone springs into action and displays the person's name or number, as well as three options: Decline Incoming Call, Answer & Hold Current Call, and Answer & End Current Call. This is part of the *call waiting* feature on your iPhone, and it's great if you're expecting an important call or if you want to add the caller to a conference call that you've set up. (Note that you only see the call waiting info if you have this feature as part of your cellular plan.)

However, the rest of the time you might just find it annoying and intrusive (and anyone you put on hold or hang up on to take the new call probably finds it rude and insulting).

Solution: You can turn off call waiting by following these steps:

1. On the Home screen, tap Settings. The Settings app appears.

2. Tap Phone. The Phone screen appears.

3. Tap Call Waiting. The Call Waiting screen appears.

4. Tap the Call Waiting switch to Off, as shown in Figure 6-6. Your iPhone disables call waiting.

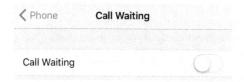

Figure 6-6. *To avoid being disturbed while on a call, turn off the Call Waiting feature*

You are Receiving Unwelcome Calls

Using your iPhone is a blast until you get your first call from a telemarketer, cold-calling salesperson, or someone similarly annoying. You might also find that you're getting unwanted calls from an old flame, an old schoolmate, or anyone else you used to know but no longer want to. One-time calls you can handle, but if you receive unwelcome calls from a person or company regularly, your iPhone becomes a lot less fun.

Solution: iOS offers a call-blocking feature that prevents specified phone numbers from calling you. Follow these steps to block a number that has recently called you:

1. Open the Phone app.

2. Tap the Recents icon in the menu bar.

3. Tap the blue Info button to the right of the phone number or person you want to block.

4. Tap Block this Caller. The Phone app asks you to confirm.

5. Tap Block Contact.

If the person you want to block isn't in the Phone app's Recents list, but they are in your Contacts list, follow these steps to block that person:

1. Open the Phone app.

2. Tap the Contacts icon in the menu bar.

3. Tap the contact you want to block.

4. Tap Block this Caller. The Phone app asks you to confirm.

5. Tap Block Contact.

> ■ **Note** To remove a person or number from the blocked list, open Settings, tap Phone, tap Call Blocking and Identification, and then tap Edit. Tap the red Delete icon to the left of the name or number, then tap Delete.

You Prefer to Answer iPhone Calls on Another Number

What do you do about incoming calls if you can't use your iPhone for a while? For example, if you're going on a flight, you must either turn off your iPhone or put it in Airplane mode so incoming calls won't go through. Similarly, if you have to return your iPhone to Apple for repairs or battery replacement, the phone won't be available if anyone tries to call you, so everything goes to voicemail.

Solution: For these and other situations where your iPhone can't accept incoming calls, you can work around the problem by having your calls forwarded to another number, such as your work or home number. Note that the availability of this feature depends on whether your cellular provider supports it.

Here's how it's done:

1. On the Home screen, tap Settings. The Settings app appears.

2. Tap Phone. The Phone screen appears.

3. Tap Call Forwarding. The Call Forwarding screen appears.

4. Tap the Call Forwarding switch to On. Your iPhone displays the Forward To screen.

5. Tap the phone number to use for the forwarded calls.

6. Tap Back to return to the Call Forwarding screen. Figure 6-7 shows the Call Forwarding screen set up to forward calls. In the status bar at the top of the screen, note the little Phone icon with an arrow that appears to the left of the time to let you know that call forwarding is on.

Figure 6-7. *Activate call forwarding to have your iPhone calls forwarded to another number*

Troubleshooting Outgoing Calls

You Want to Make a Call, but You Have Only a Few Minutes Left on Your Plan

If you're getting low on minutes with your cellular plan, the last thing you want to do is go beyond your time because those extra minutes are usually quite expensive.

Solution: You might still be able to make a call without using up what little time you have left. That's because iOS supports *Wi-Fi calling*, which enables you to place a call using a Wi-Fi Internet connection instead of a cellular connection. Check with your cellular provider to see if it supports Wi-Fi calling. If so, then you should be able to follow these steps to enable Wi-Fi calling on your iPhone:

1. On the Home screen, tap Settings. The Settings app appears.

2. Tap Phone. The Phone screen appears.

3. Tap Wi-Fi Calling. The Wi-Fi Calling screen appears.

4. Tap the Wi-Fi Calling on This iPhone switch to On, as shown in Figure 6-8. iOS asks you to confirm.

5. Tap Enable.

Figure 6-8. *Tap the Enable Wi-Fi Calling on This iPhone switch to On to make calls over Wi-Fi*

You Want to Include Extensions or Menu Options in Phone Numbers

If you're calling a family member or friend at work, or if you're phoning a particular department or person in a company, chances are you have to dial an extension after the main number connects. Similarly, many businesses require you to negotiate a series of menus to get information or connect with a particular employee or section ("Press 1 for Sales; press 2 for Customer Service," and so on). This normally requires you to display the keyboard, listen for the prompts, enter the numbers, and repeat as necessary, which is inefficient.

Solution: If you know the extension or phone menu sequence, you can program it into the number and have the Phone app do all the hard work for you. The Phone app can do either of the following:

- **Pause.** This option, which is represented by a comma (,) in the phone number, means that the Phone app dials the main number, waits for two seconds, then dials whatever extension or menu value that appears after the comma. You can add multiple commas to the number if you need a longer delay.

- **Wait.** This option, which is represented by a semicolon (;) in the phone number, means that the Phone app dials just the main number and also displays a button labeled Dial "*extension*," where *extension* is whatever digits appear after the semicolon. When the phone system prompts you to enter the extension, you tap the Dial button.

You can set these up in two ways:

- **Contacts list.** When you're entering a phone number using the Contacts list, type the full number and then tap the +*# key that appears in the lower left corner of the onscreen keyboard. This temporarily adds two new keys: pause and wait. Tap pause to add a comma, then tap the extension or menu value, and repeat as needed; tap wait to add a semicolon, and then tap the extension.

- **Keypad.** Using the keypad in the Phone app, type the full number. To add a comma to tell the Phone app to pause, tap and hold the * key until a comma appears, then tap the extension or menu value; to add a semicolon to tell the Phone app to wait, tap and hold the # key until a semicolon appears, then tap the extension.

You Don't Want to Be Identified When Making a Call

Although people often think that hiding one's calling identity is a feature only needed by miscreants and others up to no good, there are many legitimate reasons why someone might not want her identity to be revealed when making a call. Connecting with a crisis hotline, acting as a whistleblower, revealing or seeking sensitive information are all scenarios where privacy is valued, even required.

Solution: You can configure your device not to show your caller ID, assuming that feature is supported by your cellular provider. Here are the steps to follow:

1. Open the Settings app.

2. Tap Phone.

3. Tap Show My Caller ID.

4. Tap the Show My Caller ID switch to Off, as shown in Figure 6-9.

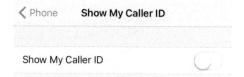

〈 Phone   **Show My Caller ID**

Show My Caller ID

Figure 6-9. *To hide your identity when calling, tap the Show My Called ID switch to Off*

■ **Caution**   You might have good reasons to hide your caller ID when making a call, but just beware that many people automatically ignore incoming calls that don't specify the caller's name.

You Want to Put a Phone Call on Hold

When you're on a call, you might want to put the caller on hold while you do something else. That's a standard phone feature, but the Phone app doesn't appear to offer it.

Solution: For reasons that remain mysterious, iOS hides this useful feature. To see it, press and hold the mute button. After several seconds, your iPhone replaces this icon with a hold icon and puts the caller on hold, as shown in Figure 6-10. To take the caller off hold, tap that icon.

Figure 6-10. *To put a phone call on hold, tap and hold the mute button for several seconds until you see the hold icon*

CHAPTER 7

■ ■ ■

Solving Problems Related to Cameras and Photos

There's a photography revolution underway, and the leader of this revolution isn't a traditional camera company such as Canon or Nikon, but a computer company. I speak, of course, of Apple and its iPhone, iPod touch, and iPad. These devices have long had cameras, but in the last generation or two those cameras have become extremely good. Add the fact that we also carry these devices with us wherever we go, and you now have hundreds of millions of people walking around with high-quality photographic equipment at hand. That is revolutionary, to say the least. And while using the camera on an iOS device doesn't come with the learning curve of, say, a digital single-lens reflex camera, it does require knowledge of how the camera works and some behind-the-scenes settings to get the most out of it and to overcome some pesky problems.

Troubleshooting Camera Problems

Many of Your Photos Are Blurry

The iOS device camera hardware is gradually getting better and the iPhone, iPad, and iPod touch generally take pretty good shots. However, probably the biggest problem most people have with iOS photos is blurry images, which are caused by not holding the device steady while taking the shot.

Solution: The iPhone 6 and later do offer optical image stabilization, which means the camera automatically compensates for subtle hand shaking and other small movements. But even if you have an earlier iPhone or some other iOS device, there are a few things you can do to minimize or hopefully eliminate blurred shots:

- Widen your stance to stabilize your body.

- Lean your shoulder (at least) or your entire side (at best) against any nearby object, such as a wall, doorframe, or car.

© Paul McFedries 2017
P. McFedries, *Troubleshooting iOS*, DOI 10.1007/978-1-4842-2445-8_7

- Place your free arm across your torso with your forearm parallel to the ground, then rest the elbow of your "shooting" arm (that is, the one holding the device) on the free arm, which should help steady your shooting arm.

- Hold your breath while taking the shot.

- Remember that your device takes the shot when you release the Shutter button, not when you press it. Therefore, keep your subject composed and yourself steadied as best you can until you lift your finger off the Shutter button.

■ **Note**   You might be tempted to press and hold the Shutter button and release it only when you're steady. Unfortunately, that technique no longer works because pressing and holding the Shutter button initiates burst mode, which takes photos at a rate of 10 per second.

- After you release the Shutter button, keep the phone steady until the photo thumbnail appears in the lower-left corner of the screen. If you move while the device is finalizing the photo, you'll blur the shot.

Keep some or all of these pointers in mind while shooting with your iOS device, and you'll soon find that blurry photos are a thing of the past.

Your Low-Light Photos Are Often Too Dark, Grainy, or Blurry

Photos taken in low-light conditions are difficult because any camera requires light, and the less light the camera has to work with, the more likely the photos will turn out too dark, too grainy, or too blurry.

The iPhone 7 Plus comes with two cameras, one of which offers a lens with an aperture of f/1.8, compared to the f/2.2 lens in the iPhone 6s and 6s Plus. In the topsy-turvy world of camera specs, a lower aperture number translates to a larger lens area – in this case, an f/1.8 lens offers 50 percent greater area than an f/2.2 lens. The greater the available lens area, the more light the camera can collect, so the better the low-light photos it can take.

Solution: If you don't have an iPhone 7 Plus, you can still take steps to improve your low-light photos. Here are some tips:

- Take advantage of any light source that's available. If you're outdoors, look for street lamps, brightly lit signs, or even a bright moon. If you're indoors and it's daytime, take your shots near a window. At night, turn on lamps and other light sources.

- Hold the device as steady as possible while shooting, particularly by using many of the same techniques I mentioned in the previous section. When the Camera app senses that there is low light available, it slows down the shutter speed – that is, keeps the shutter open longer – to allow more light to hit the lens. However, that slower shutter speed means it takes longer to expose the photo, so you're more likely to get camera shake.

■ **Tip**   For very dark conditions, consider investing in a tripod for your iOS device. This is the best way to ensure that the camera remains steady during long exposures.

- Adjust the exposure level, which controls the overall brightness of the photo. In dark conditions, the Camera app will often set the exposure to compensate, which means increasing the exposure. Unfortunately, this usually means that brighter areas of the scene get overexposed and appear washed out. Similarly, a single bright object in the scene can cause the Camera app to reduce the exposure, which can cause shadows and other dark areas to be underexposed. To adjust the exposure, compose your shot and then tap the screen to set the focus. You can now drag up on the screen to increase exposure (make the image brighter), or drag down to decrease exposure (make the image darker).

- Take advantage of the flash. Many people don't like to use the built-in camera flash because it can make subjects look washed out. But in very low-light conditions, you might not have any choice since the flash might be the only useful light source you have. The Camera app's Flash feature is set on Auto by default, meaning that the app determines whether or not it needs to use the flash. You can leave it at that, or you can set the Flash to On so that the Camera app always uses it. In the Camera app, tap the Flash icon (the lightning bolt; see Figure 7-1) and then tap either Auto or On.

Figure 7-1. *Tap Flash and then tap the setting you want to use*

- Shoot in black and white. Shadows and other darker parts of a low-light image will usually look grainy, but that grain really stands out when the photo is in color. You can improve the look of grainy parts of the photo by shooting in black and white instead of color. In the Camera app, tap the Filters icon (the three overlapping circles), and then tap one of the following filters (see Figure 7-2):

  - **Mono** — This filter converts all the colors to shades of black and white, but does no other processing. This is a good all-around filter for most low-light conditions.

  - **Tonal** — This filter is the same as Mono, except that it also increases the brightness and contrast. This is a good filter to use when it's quite dark or when there isn't much contrast in the scene.

  - **Noir** — This filter is the same as Mono, except that it also boosts a number of other levels, including the contrast, brilliance, and intensity. This can make some very dramatic photos, but you might find that some images look overprocessed.

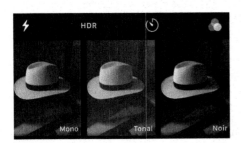

Figure 7-2. *To shoot your low-light photo in black and white, tap Filters and then tap either Mono, Tonal, or Noir*

When you're done with your low-light shooting, be sure to remove the filter by tapping the Filters icon once again, and then tapping None.

■ **Tip**   You can also apply one of the black and white filters to a photo you have already shot. Open the Photo using the Photos app; tap Edit (it's the icon that looks like a set of three equalizer bars); tap Filters; and then tap Mono, Tonal, or Noir.

You Have Trouble Keeping the Focus or Exposure Set

The Camera app offers a feature called AutoFocus, which enables the camera to automatically focus on whatever subject is in the middle of the frame.

Alternatively, you can do this yourself by tapping the screen to set the focus and exposure. If the subject you want to focus on is not in the middle of the frame, you can tap the subject and the iOS device automatically moves the focus to that object. It also automatically adjusts the white balance and exposure. If the exposure seems off, you can drag up or down anywhere on the screen to increase or decrease, respectively, the brightness.

Most people rely on AutoFocus, which is certainly a handy feature, except when you've got the perfect shot lined up and AutoFocus kicks in and wrecks the focus or exposure (or both!).

Solution: To prevent this, compose your shot and then tap and hold on the person or object you want to focus on for about three seconds (or until the focus rectangle pulses). When you release your finger, you see AE/AF Lock (short for AutoExposure/AutoFocus) at the top of the screen, as shown in Figure 7-3. Your current focus and exposure settings are now locked, meaning they won't change if you move the camera. To release the exposure and focus, tap the screen.

Figure 7-3. *To lock the exposure and focus, tap and hold the screen until you see AE/AF Lock*

You Want to Include Yourself in a Photo Taken with the Rear Camera

The term *selfie* (that is, a photo that you take of yourself, possibly with a friend or two included) was named Oxford Dictionaries' Word of the Year for 2013, which I'm sure isn't even remotely shocking news to you. You only have to look around at any event or occasion to realize that each of us has become our favorite photo subject. To make selfies even easier to shoot, just switch to the front camera, which seems nearly tailor-made for taking selfies.

I say "nearly" because the front camera method for taking selfies does come with a couple of drawbacks:

- The front camera is low resolution compared to the rear camera, and it doesn't support flash.

- All shots must be taken more or less at arm's length, which gives every such photo a characteristic "This is me taking a selfie" look.

Creative selfie-takers have worked around these limitations by using mirrors and other tricks, but iOS offers a simpler alternative: time delay. This feature tells the Camera to wait for several seconds after you tap the Shutter button before taking the photo. This means your photo-taking steps change as follows:

1. In the Camera app, use the Switch Camera icon (shown in Figure 7-4) to select the rear camera.

Figure 7-4. *Use the Camera app's Switch Camera button to choose the rear camera*

2. Tap the Time Delay button (shown in Figure 7-5) and then tap the number of seconds you want to use for the delay: 3 seconds or 10 seconds.

Figure 7-5. *In the Camera app's menu bar, tap the Time Delay icon*

3. Position your iOS device (on, say, a desk or chair) so that it's pointing toward the background that you want to use in your selfie.

4. Tap Shutter.

5. Move into the frame before the shot is taken.

Note that the Camera app takes not one photo, but a burst of 11 photos. To choose which photo you want to keep, tap the photo thumbnail in the bottom left corner, tap the photo burst, tap Select, tap the photo you want to keep, tap Done, and then tap Keep Only 1 Favorite.

■ **Tip**　Burst mode isn't only available when you're taking time-delayed photos. You can snap a burst of photos any time you want by tapping and holding the Shutter button.

You Have Trouble Taking a Straight Photo

Although you'll occasionally want to take a photo at a fun or interesting angle, most of the time our photos look their best when they're straight. However, when you're taking quick or casual shots, getting them straight can be a challenge. You can always straighten photos after you take them (see "A photo is not straight," later in this chapter), but it's better to get them straight right from the beginning.

Solution: A useful way to ensure your photos are straight is to display the Camera app's grid, which divides the frame into nine rectangles (that is, a 3x3 grid) by displaying two horizontal and two vertical lines. These lines don't show up in your photo, but you can use them to make sure your subject is aligned both horizontally and vertically. Follow these steps to activate the grid:

1. Open the Settings app.

2. Tap Photos & Camera.

3. Tap the Grid switch to On.

■ **Tip**　The grid is also useful for composing pictures using the Rule of Thirds, where you place your subject on one of the grid lines (or on the intersection of two grid lines) instead of in the middle of the screen.

Troubleshooting Photo Problems

A Photo Has the Wrong Exposure or Similar Light Problems

Even if you take quite a bit of care setting up and taking your shot, you might still end up with a photo that is under- or overexposed, has shadows that are too dark or too light, or has poor overall contrast. Of course, most of our shots are taken quickly to capture a moment, so these on-the-fly photos are even more likely to suffer from light problems.

Solution: The Photos app comes with an Enhance feature that can analyze a photo and apply several fixes automatically. Here's how to use it:

1.   In the Photos app, open the photo you want to fix.

2.   Tap the photo to display the controls, if you don't see them already.

3.   Tap Edit, shown in Figure 7-6. The Photos app displays its editing tools.

Figure 7-6. *In the Photos app's menu bar, tap Edit to load the photo editing tools*

4.   Tap Enhance (the magic wand icon in the upper-right corner; see Figure 7-7). The Photos app adjusts the color and brightness.

Figure 7-7. *To apply automatic fixes to your photo, tap the Enhance icon*

5.   Tap Done. The Photos app saves your changes.

■ **Note**   If your photo edits have made the image worse, you can restore the original. Tap to display the controls (if needed), tap Edit, tap Revert, and when Photos asks you to confirm, tap Revert to Original.

If the Enhance feature didn't improve your photo, or if you prefer a more detailed approach, the Photos app also offers editing tools that can help you solve specific problems related to light. It offers seven sliders that you can use to adjust the lighting in a photo:

- **Brilliance.** Use this slider to adjust the lighting of some parts of the photo, particularly by adjusting the lighting of the darker parts of the photo. If your photo is well exposed except for the darker parts, increase the brilliance.

- **Exposure.** Use this slider to set the overall lighting of the photo. If your entire photo is washed out because it's too light, decrease the exposure to get a darker image; if your entire photo is muddy because it's too dark, increase the exposure to get a lighter image.

- **Highlights.** Use this slider to adjust how intense the brightest parts of the image appear. If your photo has one or more areas that are washed out because they're too bright, reduce the Highlights value to counter that effect.

- **Shadows.** Use this slider to adjust how intense the darkest parts of the image appear. If your photo has one or more areas that show no detail because they're too dark, reduce the Shadows value to try and bring back some of that detail.

- **Brightness.** Use this slider to adjust all the photo's tones toward white or black. Unlike Brilliance, which mostly affects the darker parts of the photo, Brightness affects all the photo's tones. If your photo is too dark, increase the brightness; if your photo is too light, decrease the brightness.

- **Contrast.** Use this slider to adjust the distribution of the photo's tones. If the tones in your photo are starkly different, lower the contrast to make them more alike; if your photo is bland because the tones are all alike, increase the contrast to make the tones stand out.

- **Black Point.** Use this slider to set the limit for the blackest part of the image. A lower value means even the darkest parts of the image will appear gray, while a higher value means more of the photo's dark patches will appear black.

■ **Note**   Depending on your iOS device and the version of iOS on that device, you might not see all of these photo editing tools.

To adjust a photo's lighting using these tools, follow these steps:

1. In the Photos app, open the photo you want to fix.

2. Tap the photo to display the controls, if you don't see them already.

3. Tap Edit (pointed out earlier in Figure 7-6). The Photos app displays its editing tools.

4. Tap Light (see Figure 7-8).

Figure 7-8. *To apply specific light fixes to your photo, tap the Light icon*

5. Tap the Light list. (In some cases, you might need to first tap the List icon, which is similar to the icon pointed out in Figure 7-10.) The Photos app displays the available settings, as shown in Figure 7-9.

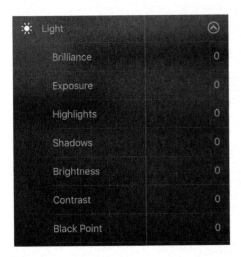

Figure 7-9. Tap the Light list to see the available light-related adjustments you can make to your photo

6. Tap the setting you want to adjust. Photos displays a slider for the setting. For example, Figure 7-10 shows the Exposure slider.

Figure 7-10. Each setting in the Light list displays a slider, such as the Exposure slider shown here

7. Drag the setting left or right until you get the look you want.

8. Tap the List icon (see Figure 7-10) to return to the Light list.

9. Repeat steps 6 to 8 to make other lighting adjustments as needed.

10. Tap Done. The Photos app saves your changes.

A Photo's Colors Look Wrong

Your photo's colors might end up looking off somehow. For example, they might lack intensity, they might look too similar, or the photo overall might look too blue or too red.

Solution: The Photos app offers several tools you can use to improve your photo's colors. The easiest of these tools is the Enhance feature, which can adjust the photo's colors automatically. To apply the Enhance tool, use the Photos app to open the photo you want to fix, tap the photo to display the controls (if you don't see them), tap Edit (shown earlier in Figure 7-6), tap Enhance (shown earlier in Figure 7-7), and then tap Done.

If the Enhance feature didn't improve your photo's colors, or if you prefer a more detailed edit, the Photos app also offers editing tools that can help you solve specific problems related to color. There are three sliders that you can use to adjust the colors in a photo:

- **Saturation.** Use this slider to adjust the intensity of the photo's colors. If your photo lacks dynamism, try increasing the saturation.

- **Contrast.** Use this slider to adjust the distribution of the photo's color tones. If the colors all kind of blend together, increase the contrast to make the colors stand apart.

- **Cast.** Use this slider to adjust a photo that has too much red or too much blue.

To adjust a photo's colors using these tools, follow these steps:

1. In the Photos app, open the photo you want to fix.

2. Tap the photo to display the controls, if you don't see them already.

3. Tap Edit (pointed out earlier in Figure 7-6). The Photos app displays its editing tools.

4. Tap Light (see Figure 7-8, earlier).

5. Tap the Color list. (In some cases, you might need to first tap the List icon, which is similar to the icon pointed out earlier in Figure 7-10.) The Photos app displays the available settings, as shown in Figure 7-11).

Figure 7-11. *Tap the Color list to see the available color-related adjustments you can make to your photo*

6. Tap the setting you want to adjust. Photos displays a slider for the setting.

7. Drag the setting left or right until you get the look you want.

8. Tap the List icon (see Figure 7-10, shown earlier) to return to the Color list.

9. Repeat steps 6 to 8 to make other color adjustments as needed.

10. Tap Done. The Photos app saves your changes.

You Think Your Black and White Photos Could Look Better

Earlier you learned that applying one of the iOS black and white photo filters — Mono, Tonal, or Noir — could improve you low-light images. Of course, you can also apply a black and white filter to any photo when you're looking for that certain starkness, simplicity, or intensity that comes with black and white. Unfortunately, it's sometimes just as likely that your black and white efforts will end up looking uninspired, bland, or messy.

Solution: It's possible that you simply picked the wrong subject, since not all scenes are suitable for the black and white treatment. Assuming that's not the case, however, you might be able to enhance your black and white photos by taking advantage of four settings in the Photos app's B&W category:

- **Intensity.** Use this slider to adjust the intensity of those parts of the photo that were converted from color to black and white. If your black and white photo lacks punch, try increasing the intensity.

- **Neutrals.** Use this slider to adjust the intensity of those parts of the photo that were converted from white or a shade of gray. If those parts of your black and white aren't prominent, try increasing the neutral value.

- **Tone.** Use this slider to adjust the overall intensity of the photo. If your black and white photo looks washed out, try increasing the tone.

- **Grain.** Use this slider to add graininess to your photo. If you want your photo to have a vintage look, try increasing the grain.

To adjust a black and white photo using these tools, follow these steps:

1. In the Photos app, open the photo you want to fix.

2. Tap the photo to display the controls, if you don't see them already.

3. Tap Edit (pointed out earlier in Figure 7-6). The Photos app displays its editing tools.

4. Tap Light (see Figure 7-8, earlier).

5. Tap the B&W list. (In some cases, you might need to first tap the List icon, which is similar to the icon pointed out earlier in Figure 7-10.) The Photos app displays the available settings, as shown in Figure 7-12).

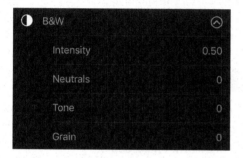

Figure 7-12. Tap the B&W list to see the available black and white-related adjustments you can make to your photo

6. Tap the setting you want to adjust. Photos displays a slider for the setting.

7. Drag the setting left or right until you get the look you want.

8. Tap the List icon (see Figure 7-10, shown earlier) to return to the B&W list.

9. Repeat steps 6 to 8 to make other black and white adjustments as needed.

10. Tap Done. The Photos app saves your changes.

A Photo Contains One or More Instances of Red-Eye

When you use a flash to take a picture of one or more people or animals, in some cases the flash may reflect off the subjects' retinas. The result is the common phenomenon of red-eye, where the subject's pupils appear red instead of black.

Solution: If you have a photo on your iOS device where one or more people or animals have red-eye due to the camera flash, you can use the Photos app to remove it and give your subjects a more natural look. Here's how:

1. In the Photos app, open the photo that contains the red-eye you want to remove.

2. Tap the photo to display the controls, if you don't see them already.

3. Tap Edit (pointed out earlier in Figure 7-6). The Photos app displays its editing tools.

4. Tap Red-Eye, shown in Figure 7-13.

Figure 7-13. *Tap the Red-Eye icon to display the Photos app's red-eye removal tool*

5. Tap the red-eye that you want to remove. The Photos app removes the red-eye.

6. Repeat Step 5 until you've removed all the red-eye in the photo.

7. Tap Done. The Photos app applies the changes to the photo.

A Photo Contains Elements You Want to Remove

When you frame a scene before taking a photo, you likely try to avoid certain elements that could detract from the final image, such as a light pole or the top of the fence over which you're shooting. Despite your best efforts, you'll find that it's not uncommon to see unwanted parts of the scene in your photo.

Solution: When you have a photo containing elements that you do not want or need to see, you can often cut them out. This is called *cropping* and you can use the Photos app to do it. When you crop a photo, you specify a rectangular area of the image that you want to keep. The Photos app then discards everything outside of the rectangle. Cropping is a useful skill for removing extraneous elements that appear on or near the edges of a photo, but you can also use it to help you give prominence to the true subject of a photo.

Follow these steps to crop a photo:

1. In the Photos app, open the photo that you want to crop.

2. Tap the photo to display the controls, if you don't see them already.

3. Tap Edit (pointed out earlier in Figure 7-6). The Photos app displays its editing tools.

4. Tap Crop & Straighten (shown in Figure 7-14). The Photos app displays a grid for cropping, as shown in Figure 7-15.

Figure 7-14. *Tap the Crop & Straighten icon to display the Photos app's cropping tool*

Figure 7-15. *Tap and drag the corners to crop the photo*

5. Tap and drag a corner of the grid to set the area you want to keep.

6. Tap Done. The Photos app applies the changes to the photo.

■ **Tip** The fastest way to crop some photos is to tell the Photos app the dimensions you want to use for the resulting photo. Tap Aspect (pointed out in Figure 7-14), and then tap either a specific shape (Original or Square) or a specific ratio, such as 5:7 or 4:5. You then drag the photo (not the grid!) so the portion you want to keep is within the grid.

A Photo Is Not Straight

As you probably know from hard-won experience, getting an iPhone camera perfectly level when you take a shot is very difficult. It requires a lot of practice and a steady hand. (You can also activate the Camera app's grid feature; see the section "You Have Trouble Taking a Straight Photo.") Despite your best efforts, you might still end up with a photo that is not quite level.

Solution: To fix this problem, you can use the Photos app to rotate the photo clockwise or counterclockwise so that the subject appears straight. Follow these steps to crop and straighten a photo:

1. In the Photos app, open the photo that you want to straighten.

2. Tap the photo to display the controls, if you don't see them already.

3. Tap Edit (pointed out earlier in Figure 7-6). The Photos app displays its editing tools.

4. Tap Crop & Straighten (see Figure 7-14). The Photos app displays the Straightening tool (the arc with the degree markings; see Figure 7-15).

5. Drag the Straightening tool left or right until the photo is level.

6. Tap Done. The Photos app applies the changes to the photo.

■ **Note** The Crop & Straighten feature also enables you to rotate a photo 90 degrees, say, from portrait to landscape. To do this, tap the Rotate icon (see Figure 7-14) until the photo is in the orientation you want.

CHAPTER 8

■ ■ ■

Protecting Your Device

The iPhone has only been around since 2007, and the iPad since 2010, but already these devices have become indispensable parts of many people's lives. That indispensability comes from the sheer versatility of these devices. In a typical day, you probably use your iOS device to surf the Web, exchange emails and text messages, make calls, manage your contacts and calendar, listen to music, play games, check the weather or the stock market, and a dozen other tasks large and small. However, that insanely great power and convenience come with a price: your iOS device is loaded with information about you. To be sure, most of that data is likely trivial or ephemeral, but much of it is private and sensitive. Losing your iOS device would be a major inconvenience, but someone else getting access to your information could lead to big problems. So, yes, the notion of protecting your iOS device might not sound like a troubleshooting topic. But taking steps to ensure that you can find your device if it gets lost, and that while your device is lost no one else can see or mess with your information, can be viewed as a form of preventative maintenance. And preventing trouble before it happens is the best type of troubleshooting.

Locking Your Device

When your iOS device is asleep, it's locked in the sense that tapping the touchscreen or pressing the volume controls does nothing. This sensible arrangement prevents accidental taps when the phone is in your pocket, or rattling around in your backpack or handbag. To unlock the device, you either press the Home button twice, or press the Sleep/Wake button and then the Home button. Just like that, you're back in business.

Unfortunately, this simple technique means that anyone else who gets his or her hands on your iOS device can also be quickly back in business – your business! If you have sensitive or confidential information on your device, or if you want to avoid digital joyrides that run up massive roaming or data charges, you need to truly lock your iOS device.

© Paul McFedries 2017
P. McFedries, *Troubleshooting iOS*, DOI 10.1007/978-1-4842-2445-8_8

You Want to Lock Your Device with a Passcode

In the same way that you "lock" your user account and your many online accounts with a password, you might prefer to lock your iOS device with something similar.

Solution: You can do that by specifying a *passcode* that must be entered before anyone can use the device. The default in iOS is a six-digit passcode, but you can change that to either a simple four-digit passcode, or to a custom code that is longer and more complex and uses any combination of numbers, letters, and symbols.

Follow these steps to set up your passcode:

1. On the Home screen, tap Settings. The Settings app appears.

2. Tap Touch ID & Passcode to open the Touch ID & Passcode screen. If your iOS device doesn't support Touch ID, tap Passcode, instead, to open the Passcode Lock screen.

3. Tap Turn Passcode On. The Set Passcode screen appears.

4. If you prefer to use something other than a six-digit passcode, tap Passcode Options and then tap the type of passcode you want to use (see Figure 8-1).

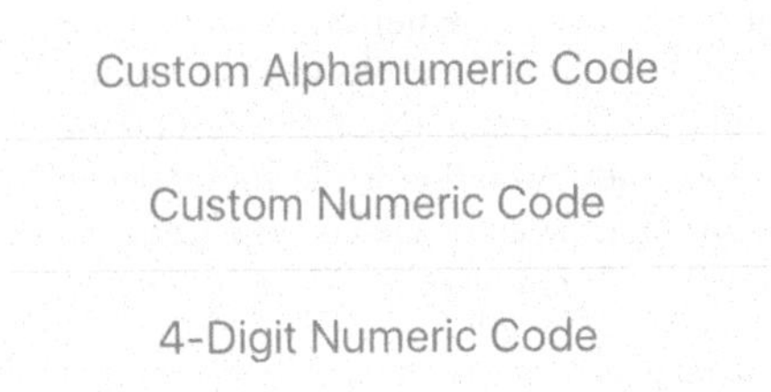

Custom Alphanumeric Code

Custom Numeric Code

4-Digit Numeric Code

Figure 8-1. *iOS gives you several options for the type of passcode you want to use*

5. Tap your passcode. For security, the characters appear in the passcode box as dots.

6. If you're entering a custom passcode, tap Next. Your iOS device prompts you to reenter the passcode.

7. Tap your passcode again.

8. If you're entering a custom passcode, tap Done.

■ **Caution** You really, really need to remember your iOS device passcode. If you forget it, you're locked out of your own device. The only way to get back in is to use iTunes to restore the data and settings to your iOS device from an existing backup (as described in Chapter 1).

You Want to Guarantee That Your Data Won't Fall into Malicious Hands

If your iOS device falls into another person's hands, your passcode will prevent that person from accessing your data and apps. You might be wondering what happens when that person tries guessing the password:

- After six failed passcodes, iOS locks the device — that is, prevents any further passcode attempts — for one minute, as shown in Figure 8-2.

Figure 8-2. After a person tries to guess your passcode six times incorrectly, iOS prevents further attempts for one minute

- After a seventh failed attempt, iOS locks the device for five minutes.

- After an eighth failed attempt, iOS locks the device for fifteen minutes.

- After a ninth failed attempt, iOS locks the device for one hour.

- After a tenth failed attempt, iOS locks the device completely and you must sync with iTunes to restore your data.

If your device contains extremely sensitive or private data, you might be concerned that someone could still somehow access the data.

Solution: You can configure your iOS device to not only lock completely after the tenth failed passcode attempt, but also to erase all of its data. Here's how to set this up:

1. On the Home screen, tap Settings. The Settings app appears.

2. Tap Touch ID & Passcode. If your iOS device doesn't support Touch ID, tap Passcode, instead. iOS prompts you to enter your passcode.

3. Type your passcode and, if you're using a custom passcode, tap Done.

4. Tap the Erase Data switch to On. iOS asks you to confirm that you want to enable this feature.

5. Tap Enable. iOS enables Erase Data, as shown in Figure 8-3.

Erase Data

Erase all data on this iPhone after 10 failed passcode attempts.

Figure 8-3. With Erase Data enabled, your iOS device automatically erases all of its data after it detects ten consecutive failed passcodes

You Need to Make an Emergency Call While Your iPhone Is Locked

If an emergency arises and you need to make a call for help, you probably don't want to mess around with entering a passcode. Similarly, if something happens to you, another person who doesn't know your passcode may need to use your iPhone device to call for assistance.

Solution: In both cases, you can temporarily bypass the passcode by tapping the Emergency button on the Enter Passcode screen, shown in Figure 8-4.

Figure 8-4. In the Enter Passcode screen, you can tap Emergency to make an emergency phone call without unlocking the iPhone

You Are Using a Passcode, but It Does Not Always Appear When You Unlock Your Device

By default, iOS puts the passcode into effect as soon as you lock your device, or as soon as the device locks itself after a period of inactivity. This is a sensible default because your passcode cannot protect your device if your device is unlocked. However, you might find that you can lock your device and iOS does not request the passcode when you unlock it.

Solution: This problem means that your iOS device has been configured to not require a passcode immediately after it has been locked. Some people set up the passcode to not kick in until the device has been locked for at least one minute to avoid having to constantly retype the passcode each the device locks itself due to inactivity. However, any delay in requiring the passcode makes your device that much less secure.

To ensure that the passcode is required as soon as your iOS device is locked, follow these steps:

1. On the Home screen, tap Settings. The Settings app appears.

2. Tap Touch ID & Passcode. If your iOS device doesn't support Touch ID, tap Passcode, instead. iOS prompts you to enter your passcode.

3. Type your passcode and, if you're using a custom passcode, tap Done.

4. Tap the Require Passcode to open the Require Passcode screen.

5. Tap Immediately, as shown in Figure 8-5.

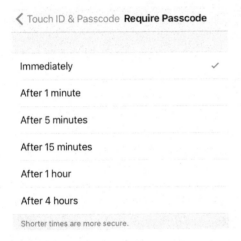

Figure 8-5. *To ensure that your passcode is always protecting your locked device, set the Require Passcode setting to Immediately*

You Want to Be Able to Unlock Your Device with Your Fingerprint

Protecting your iOS device with a passcode is just good sense in this age of so-called iCrime, where thieves routinely go "Apple picking" by snatching iPhones and other Apple devices from the unwary. With a passcode acting as a digital barrier between the crook and your iOS device, at least your personal data is safe from prying eyes. Yes, a passcode is a smart safety precaution, but it's not always a convenient one. First, having to tap that four (or more) character code many times during the day adds a small but nevertheless unwelcome annoyance to using the device. Second, because iOS, perhaps unwisely, highlights each character as you type your passcode, it's at least theoretically possible that some shoulder-surfing snoop could discern your code.

Solution: If you have an iOS device that supports Touch ID — that is, if you have an iPhone 5s or later, an iPad Pro, an iPad Air 2, or an iPad mini 3 or later — you can take advantage of Touch ID, the fingerprint sensor built into the Home button of these iOS devices. By teaching the device your unique fingerprint, you can unlock your device merely by pressing the Home button. That's right: No more passcode tapping to get to your Home screen. As an added bonus, you can use the same fingerprint to approve purchases you make in the iTunes Store, the App Store, the iBooks Store, Apple Pay, and even some third-party apps, so you no longer have to enter your Apple ID password.

Here's how to set up Touch ID:

1. On the Home screen, tap Settings. The Settings app appears.

2. Tap Touch ID & Passcode and then type your passcode (if you have one) to open the Touch ID & Passcode screen.

3. Tap Add a Fingerprint. The Touch ID screen appears.

4. Lightly rest your thumb – or whatever finger you most often use to press the Home button when you're unlocking your iOS device – on the Home button.

5. Repeatedly lift and place your finger as Touch ID learns your fingerprint pattern.

6. When you see the Adjust Your Grip screen, tap Continue.

7. Once again, repeatedly lift and place your finger, this time emphasizing the edges of the finger.

8. When you see the Complete screen, tap Continue. If you haven't yet specified a passcode, your iOS device prompts you to do so now.

9. Tap your passcode and then tap it again when you're asked to confirm. Settings returns you to the Touch ID & Passcode screen.

10. To specify another fingerprint, repeat Steps 3 to 8.

You Can't Unlock Your iOS Device Using Your Fingerprint

Using Touch ID to unlock your iOS device is a major convenience, particularly if you'd otherwise have to enter a custom numeric or alphanumeric passcode that's fairly long. However, that convenience goes out the window if your iOS devices refuses to unlock when you apply your finger to the Home button.

Solution: There are a number of reasons why you can't unlock your iOS device using your fingerprint:

- If your device is running iOS 10, remember that you might have to unlock the device by *pressing* the Home button with the digit that you saved as a fingerprint. On some devices, and in earlier versions of iOS, you unlocked the device by *resting* that finger on the Home button.

- Touch ID does not work if you've just restarted your device or if you haven't unlocked the device in the last 48 hours. In these cases, iOS forces you to use your passcode to unlock the device. iOS also insists on a passcode if your fingerprint isn't recognized after five consecutive tries.

- Make sure you're using a digit that has been added to iOS as a Touch ID fingerprint. It's not unusual for people to add, say, a right thumb or forefinger and then try to unlock the device using the left thumb or forefinger.

- Make sure your finger completely covers the Home button.

- Do not move your finger while it's on the Home button.

- Make sure your finger is clean and dry.

- Touch ID will sometimes fail if your finger is very cold, so try warming up the finger.

- Make sure your finger doesn't have any cuts or swelling.

- If you have recently been swimming or in the shower, your finger might have absorbed enough water to change its print (resulting in so-called *raisin fingers*). In this case, you have no choice but to wait until the fingerprint returns to its normal state.

- Use a soft cloth to clean the Home button.

- Make sure a case or other protective covering isn't obscuring part of the Home button.

- Make sure iOS is configured to unlock the device using a fingerprint. Run the Settings app, tap Touch ID & Passcode, then type your passcode to open the Touch ID & Passcode screen. Make sure the *Device* Unlock switch (where *Device* is iPhone or iPad) is set to On, as shown in Figure 8-6.

Figure 8-6. *To unlock your device using a saved fingerprint, make sure the Device Unlock switch is On*

If none of these solutions work for you, then you should delete all your fingerprints and add them again. Follow these steps to delete fingerprints:

1. On the Home screen, tap Settings. The Settings app appears.

2. Tap Touch ID & Passcode and then type your passcode to open the Touch ID & Passcode screen.

3. Tap the fingerprint you want to remove.

4. Tap Delete Fingerprint. iOS deletes the fingerprint and returns you to the Touch ID & Passcode screen.

5. Repeat steps 3 and 4 to remove all your fingerprints.

■ **Tip** An easier way to delete a fingerprint is to follow steps 1 and 2, swipe left on the fingerprint, and then tap the Delete button that appears.

You Don't Want to Forget Which Fingerprint You've Configured for Touch ID

If you don't use Touch ID that often, it's possible that you might forget which finger or fingers you've added as fingerprints in iOS.

Solution: To help you remember, you can provide a descriptive name for each fingerprint (such as "Right thumb" or "Left forefinger"). Here's how you do this:

1. On the Home screen, tap Settings. The Settings app appears.

2. Tap Touch ID & Passcode and then type your passcode to open the Touch ID & Passcode screen.

3. Tap a saved fingerprint (which will have a generic name such as "Finger 1").

■ **Tip**   If iOS has given your fingerprints generic names such as "Finger 1" and "Finger 2," how do you know which is which? With the Touch ID & Passcode screen displayed, rest a finger on the Home button. If iOS recognizes that finger, it highlights the corresponding fingerprint name.

---

4.   Type a new name for the fingerprint, as shown in Figure 8-7 and then tap Done.

5.   Repeat steps 3 and 4 for each saved fingerprint.

Figure 8-7. To help you remember which digits you've added as fingerprints, supply each fingerprint with a descriptive name

You Want to Configure Your Device to Lock Automatically

You can lock your iOS device at any time by pressing the Sleep/Wake button once. However, if your iOS device is on but you're not using it, it automatically goes into standby mode after two minutes. This is called Auto-Lock and it's a handy feature because it saves battery power (and prevents accidental taps) when your iOS device is just sitting there. It's also a crucial feature if you've protected your iOS device with a passcode or fingerprint lock, as I describe earlier, because if your iOS device is never locked, then these security features are useless. You might find, however, that your iOS device does not lock itself automatically after a period of inactivity.

Solution: To make sure your iOS device locks automatically, you must configure the Auto-Lock feature to shut of the device after a specified period of inactivity. Here are the steps to follow:

1.   On the Home screen, tap Settings. The Settings app appears.

2.   In iOS 10, tap Display & Brightness. In earlier versions of iOS, tap General.

3.   Tap Auto-Lock. The Auto-Lock screen appears.

4.   Tap the interval you want to use. Note that the available options depend on your device. Figure 8-8 shows the options available for the iPhone: 30 seconds, 1 Minute, 2 Minutes, 3 Minutes, 4 Minutes, or 5 Minutes.

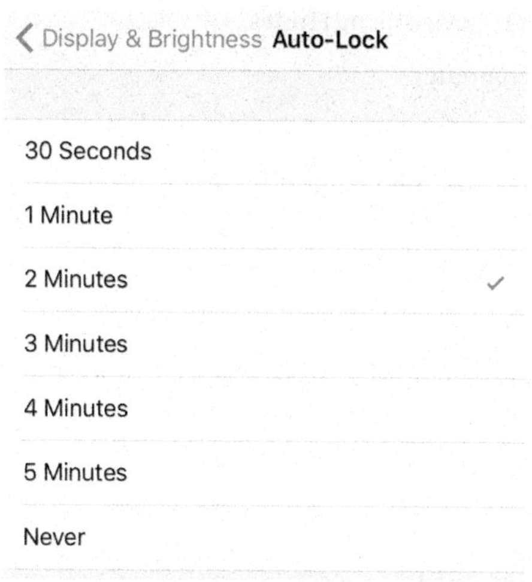

⟨ Display & Brightness **Auto-Lock**

30 Seconds	
1 Minute	
2 Minutes	✓
3 Minutes	
4 Minutes	
5 Minutes	
Never	

Figure 8-8. *To ensure your passcode and/or fingerprint lock can do their jobs, use Auto-Lock to automatically lock your device after it has been inactive for the specified time*

Backing Up Your Device

If something bad happens to your iOS device – for example, it crashes and will no longer start normally, it gets damaged or lost, or you forget your passcode – you can get back on your feet by restoring the device's default settings (as described in Chapter 1). What about all that data you've stored on your device? To restore that, you need to have a backup available, either on your computer or on iCloud.

You Want to Back Up Your Device without Syncing

When you sync your iOS device with your computer, iTunes automatically creates a backup of your current iOS device data before performing the sync. Note, however, that iTunes doesn't back up your entire iOS device, which makes sense because most of what's on your device @@md music, photos, videos, apps, and so on @@md is already on your computer. Instead, iTunes backs up only data unique to the iOS device, including your call history, text messages, web clips, network settings, app settings and data, and Safari history and cookies.

However, if you've configured iTunes not to sync your iOS device automatically, you might want to back up your iOS device without performing a sync.

Solution: Follow these steps to back up your iOS device using iTunes:

1. Connect your iOS device to your computer.

2. Open iTunes, if it doesn't launch automatically.

3. If your iOS device asks whether you trust this computer, tap Trust and, on your computer, click Continue.

4. In the Devices list, click your iOS device.

5. Click the Summary tab.

6. Click Back Up Now, as shown in Figure 8-9. iTunes backs up the iOS device data.

Figure 8-9. *In iTunes, click your connected iOS device, click the Summary tab, and then click Back Up Now*

You Want iOS to Back Up your Device Automatically

Using iTunes to back up your iOS device is handy, but it requires that you connect your device to your computer, open iTunes, and run the backup. These are not onerous steps, but they present enough of a hurdle that you might not back up your device regularly. That's a problem because they key to restoring your data successfully should it come to that is to have a recent backup available.

To make sure this happens, it would be nice to have a way to automatically back up your iOS device on a regular schedule.

Solution: If you have an iCloud account, you can configure your iOS device to use iCloud as the backup location.

If you regularly use iTunes to sync your iOS device, you can tell iTunes to use iCloud as the backup location. To configure this, follow these steps:

1. Connect your iOS device to your computer.

2. In iTunes, click your iOS device when it appears in the Devices list.

3. Click the Summary tab.

4. In the Automatically Back Up section, select iCloud, as shown in Figure 8-10.

Figure 8-10. *In iTunes, click your connected iOS device, click the Summary tab, and then click iCloud in the Automatically Back Up section*

If you never use iTunes, you can still configure iOS to back up your data to iCloud directly from your iOS device:

1. On the Home screen, tap Settings to launch the Settings app.

2. Tap iCloud.

3. Tap Backup.

4. Tap the iCloud Backup switch to On, as shown in Figure 8-11, and then tap OK when iCloud confirms the setting. This tells iOS to make automatic backups whenever the device is locked, connected to a Wi-Fi network, and plugged in to a power source.

Figure 8-11. *Tap iCloud Backup to On to set up automatic iCloud backups*

5. To run a backup right away, tap Back Up Now. Your iOS device backs up its data to your iCloud account.

You're Having iCloud Backup Problems

After you've set up iCloud backups, you might find that the backups don't complete or don't run at all.

Solution: There are a number of possible reasons why iCloud backups won't run. Here are some things to look for:

- Make sure that iCloud backups are activated. Open the Settings app, tap iCloud, tap Backup, and then tap the iCloud Backup switch to On.

- Make sure your iOS device is connected to a Wi-Fi network. iCloud backups do not work if there is no Internet connection, nor do they work over a cellular connection.

- Make sure your iOS device is plugged in to a power source.

- Make sure your device is locked.

- Check that you have free space on your iCloud account. To check this, open the Settings app, tap iCloud, and then examine the Available value beside the Storage command, as shown in Figure 8-12.

Storage	12.8 GB Available >

Figure 8-12. In the Settings app's iCloud screen, the Storage command shows you how much free space is left in your iCloud account

---

■ **Note**   How do you know whether you have enough free space on iCloud? Backup size varies according to device and capacity, but expect your backup to require anywhere from 400 MB to 1 GB.

If your iCloud backup is failing because storage space is low, you can free up some space by deleting one or more backups from devices you no long own or use:

1. On the Home screen, tap Settings to launch the Settings app.

2. Tap iCloud.

3. Tap Storage.

4. Tap Manage Storage.

5. In the Backups section, tap the device whose backups you want to delete.

6. Tap Delete Backup. iOS asks you to confirm that you want to turn off backups for this device and delete its backup data.

7. Tap Turn Off & Delete.

Protecting a Lost Device

If there's a downside to using an iOS device, it's that you end up with a pretty large chunk of your life on that device. Initially, that may sound like a good thing, but if you happen to lose your device, you've also lost that chunk of your life. Plus, assuming you haven't configured your iOS device with a passcode lock, as described earlier, you've opened a gaping privacy hole because anyone can now delve into your data.

If you've been backing up your iOS device regularly, then you can probably recover most, or even all, of that data. However, I'm sure you'd probably rather find your device because it's expensive and there's just something creepy about the thought of some stranger flicking through your stuff.

The old way of finding your missing iOS device consisted of scouring every nook and cranny that you visited before losing it, and calling up various lost-and-found departments to see if anyone turned it in. The new way to find your iOS device is via a feature called Find My iPhone. (You can use this feature through your iCloud account, if you have one, or through the Find My iPhone app.) Find My iPhone uses the GPS sensor embedded inside your iOS device to locate the device. You can also use Find My iPhone to play a sound on your iOS device, remotely lock it and send a message, or, in a real pinch, remotely delete your data.

■ **Note**   You might think that a fatal flaw with Find My iPhone is that someone who has your iOS device can easily turn off the feature and disable it. Fortunately, that's not the case because iOS comes with a feature called Activation Lock, which means that a person can turn off Find My iPhone only by entering your Apple ID password.

You Want to Ensure That You Can Find a Lost Device

Find My iPhone works by looking for a particular signal that your iOS device beams out into the ether. This signal is turned off by default, so you need to turn it on if you ever plan to use Find My iPhone.

Solution: Follow these steps to activate Find My iPhone:

1. On the Home screen, tap Settings. The Settings app appears.

2. Tap iCloud. Your iCloud account settings appear.

3. Tap Find My *Device* (where *Device* is iPhone, iPad, or iPod).

4. Tap the Find My *Device* switch to On. iOS asks you to confirm.

5. Tap Allow.

■ **Tip**   Your lost iOS device might just be lying somewhere where no one can find it. In that case, the danger is that the iOS device battery will die before you have a chance to locate it using Find My iPhone. To make this less likely, be sure to activate the Send Last Location switch. This configures iOS to send you the device's last known location as soon as it detects that its battery is nearly done.

You Want to Locate a Lost Device on a Map

To get a general idea of where your lost device is located, you might prefer to see its location visually, by using a map.

Solution: You can use the Find My iPhone feature of icloud.com to locate your device. Here are the steps to follow:

1.   Use a web browser to navigate to www.icloud.com.

■ **Note**   Rather than using icloud.com, you can also use the Find My iPhone app to locate your lost iOS device.

2.   Sign in to your iCloud account.

3.   Click Find My iPhone. The iCloud Find My iPhone application appears.

4.   Click All Devices. iCloud displays a list of your iOS devices.

5.   Click your lost iOS device in the list. iCloud locates your iOS device on a map, as shown in Figure 8-13.

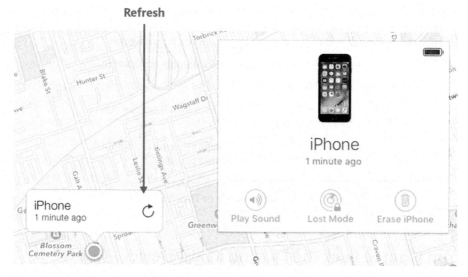

Figure 8-13. *You can use iCloud's Find My iPhone application to locate your lost iOS device on a map*

▓ **Tip** To see if the device's location has changed, click the Refresh Location button (pointed out in Figure 8-13).

You Want to Locate a Lost Device by Playing a Sound

Locating your lost device on a map is often handy (for example, it might show you that your device is in your house or your workplace), but most of the time it's not specific enough to tell you exactly where your device can be found.

If you misplace your iPhone, the first thing you should try is calling your number using another device so you can hear it ringing.

The solution won't work if, for example, your phone has Ring/Silent switched to silent mode, if it's in Airplane mode, or if you don't have another device handy. It would be nice to be able to hear a sound on your iPhone anyway, and it would be nice to be able to hear a sound on a lost iPad or iPod touch.

Solution: You can use Find My iPhone to play a sound on your device. This sound plays even if your iOS device is in silent mode or Airplane mode, and it plays loudly even if your iOS device has its volume turned down or muted. Here's how it works:

1. Sign in to iCloud and open the Find My iPhone application.

2. Display the My Devices list.

3. Click your lost iOS device in the list. Find My iPhone locates your iOS device on a map.

4. Click Play Sound. Find My iPhone begins playing the sound on your iOS device and displays an alert message.

5. When you find your iOS device, tap OK in the alert message (and, if needed, enter your passcode or Touch ID) to silence the sound.

You Want to Lock the Data on a Lost Device

If you can't find your iOS device right away by playing a sound, your next step should be to ensure that some other person who finds the device can't rummage around in your stuff.

Solution: You do that by putting your iOS device into *lost mode*, which remotely locks the iOS device using the passcode that you set earlier. (If you didn't protect your iOS device with a passcode, you can't remotely lock the device.) You can also provide a phone number where you can be reached and send a message for whoever finds your iOS device.

Follow these steps to put your iOS device into lost mode:

1. Sign in to iCloud and open the Find My iPhone application.

2. Display the My Devices list.

3. Click your lost iOS device in the list. Find My iPhone locates the device on a map.

4. Click Lost Mode. Find My iPhone displays the Lost Mode dialog, which prompts you for a phone number where you can be reached.

5. Type your phone number and then click Next. Find My iPhone prompts you to type a message that will appear on the iOS device along with the phone number.

6. Type the message and then tap or click Done. Find My iPhone remotely locks the iOS device and displays the message.

■ **Caution**   If you do not locate your device after it has been locked, keep an eye out for an email or text message telling you that your device has been found. When you click the link, you're asked to provide your Apple sign-in credentials. This will look like a legitimate Apple message, but it's really a scam set up to obtain your Apple ID sign-in data, so that the scammer can unlock your device.

You Want to Erase the Data on a Lost Device

If you can't get the other person to return your iOS device and it contains sensitive or confidential data, you might want to take further steps to ensure that the other person cannot access your data.

Solution: You can use Find My iPhone to take the drastic step of remotely wiping all the data from your iOS device. Here are the steps to follow:

1. Sign in to iCloud and open the Find My iPhone application.

2. Display the My Devices list.

3. Click your lost iOS device in the list. Find My iPhone locates the device on a map.

4. Click Erase *Device* (where *Device* is iPhone, iPad, or iPod). Find My iPhone prompts you for your Apple ID password.

5. Type your password and then click Next. Find My iPhone asks you to enter an optional phone number where you can be reached, which will appear on the iOS device after it has been erased.

6. Type your phone number, and then click Next. Find My iPhone prompts you to type a message that will appear on the iOS device along with the phone number, after it has been erased.

7. Type the message, and then click Done. Find My iPhone remotely wipes all data from the iOS device.

■ **Note**   If you locate your device after you have erased it, you can restore your settings, apps, and data by connecting the device to your computer and then using iTunes to restore your most recent backup.

CHAPTER 9

■ ■ ■

Solving Privacy Problems

One of the unforeseen consequences of the mobile device revolution is that we now often do our computing in public. Yes, there have long been people tapping on laptops in coffee shops, but these days we're more likely to also be tapping on our phones and tablets on buses, in parks, before movies, and after classes. This means that privacy is a potential problem because now people can see our screens as we work. Another unforeseen consequence of the mobile device revolution is that we now carry with us a great deal of personal or confidential information. This opens up another potential privacy problem because if someone gained access to your device, that person would be free to view your apps, your oft-visited locations, your browsing history, and much more. In Chapter 8 you learned how to lock your iOS device, but it isn't difficult to imagine scenarios where someone could still access your device while it is unlocked. All this means that it's important to take privacy seriously and to embrace a prudent paranoia: Assume someone is watching your screen when you're in public; assume someone could gain unlocked access to your device. This chapter shows you how to take steps to solve these and similar privacy problems.

Troubleshooting General Privacy Issues

Let's begin by troubleshooting a few issues related to general privacy concerns,

As You Type, Each Character Pops Up on the Screen, Creating a Privacy Risk

The iPhone onscreen keyboard comes with a feature called character preview, which displays a pop-up version of each character as you tap it. (This doesn't happen on the iPad.) This is great for iOS keyboard rookies because it helps them be sure they're typing accurately, but veterans often find it distracting. Either way, it's a potential privacy risk to have each character pop up when you're typing where anyone nearby can see your screen.

© Paul McFedries 2017
P. McFedries, *Troubleshooting iOS*, DOI 10.1007/978-1-4842-2445-8_9

Solution: Apple chose to turn off character preview by default in iOS 9, but if you're seeing characters as you type on your iPhone, then you need to turn it off yourself by following these steps:

1. Open the Settings app.

2. Tap General.

3. Tap Keyboard.

4. Tap the Character Preview switch to Off, as shown in Figure 9-1.

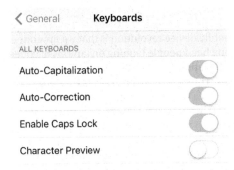

Figure 9-1. *To prevent characters from popping up as your type them, turn off the Character Preview setting*

■ **Caution**   Even with Character Preview set to On, iOS no longer shows pop-up versions of password characters. That's nice, but it still shows your most recently tapped password character for as long as three seconds! There's no way to turn that off, so try to cover your password typing when you're in a public place.

You Want to Stop an App from Using Another App's Data

Third-party apps occasionally request permission to use the data from another app. For example, an app might need access to your contacts, your calendars, your photos, or your Twitter and Facebook accounts. You can always deny these requests, of course, but if you've allowed access to an app in the past, you might later change your mind and decide you'd prefer to revoke that access.

Solution: iOS offers a privacy feature that enables you to control which apps have access to your data. Here's how it works:

1. Open the Settings app.

2. Tap Privacy. The Privacy screen appears.

3. Tap the app or feature for which you want to control access. iOS displays a list of third-party apps that have requested access to the app or feature. Figure 9-2 shows an example for the Photos app.

Figure 9-2. *In Settings, tap Privacy and then tap an app or feature to see the third-party apps that have requested access to that item*

4. To revoke a third-party app's access to the app or feature, tap its switch to Off.

You Do Not Want Your Location Tracked

In iOS, *location services* refers to the features and technologies that provide apps and system tools with access to the current geographical coordinates of the device. This is a handy thing, but it's also something that you need to keep under your control because your location data, particularly your current location, is fundamentally private and shouldn't be given out willy-nilly. Fortunately, iOS comes with a few tools for controlling and configuring location services.

The next couple of sections show you how to turn off location services for individual apps as well as individual system services. That fine-grained control is the best way to handle location services, but there may be times when you prefer a broader approach that turns off location services altogether. For example, if you're heading to a secret rendezvous (how exciting!) and you're bringing your iOS device with you, you might feel more comfortable knowing that no app or service on your device is tracking your whereabouts.

■ **Note** On a more mundane level, location services use up battery power, so if your iOS device is getting low or if you just want to maximize the battery (for a long bus ride, for example), then turning off location services completely will help.

Solution: Follow these steps to turn off all location services on your iOS device:

1. Open the Settings app.

2. Tap Privacy. The Privacy settings appear.

3. Tap Location Services. The Location Services settings appear.

4. Tap the Location Services switch to the Off position. iOS asks you to confirm.

5. Tap Turn Off. iOS shuts off all location services (see Figure 9-3).

Figure 9-3. *To prevent your location from being used by any app or service, set the Location Services switch to Off*

You Want to Stop an App from Using Your Location

When you open an app that comes with a GPS component, the app displays a dialog like the one shown in Figure 9-4 to ask your permission to use the GPS hardware in your device to determine your current location. Notice that iOS only allows apps to access your location while you use the app. Once you exit the app, it can no longer access your location. Tap Don't Allow if you think that your current location is none of the app's business, or tap Allow if that's just fine with you.

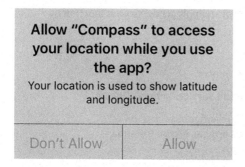

Figure 9-4. *When you first launch a GPS-aware app, it asks your permission to access your current location while you use the app*

A slightly different scenario is when an app must use your location to function. A good example is Foursquare, which requires your location to show you nearby businesses and to let you "check in" to those places. In this case, iOS automatically gives the app access to your location while you're using the app, but the app might request access to your location even when you're not using it, as shown in Figure 9-5. Again, tap Don't Allow if you think the app is overstepping its bounds, or tap Allow if it's all good.

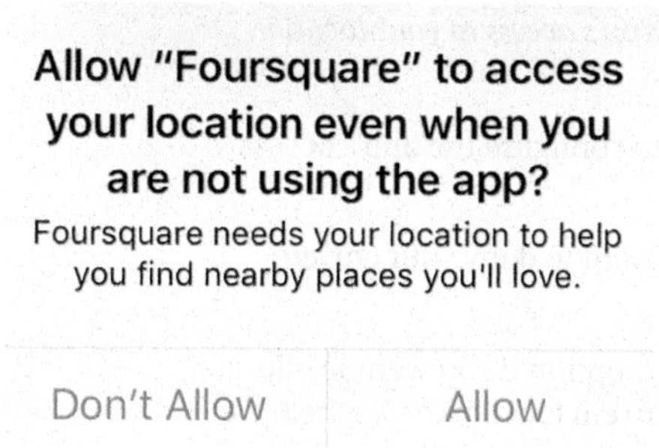

Allow "Foursquare" to access your location even when you are not using the app?
Foursquare needs your location to help you find nearby places you'll love.

Don't Allow   Allow

Figure 9-5. *An app that must access your location while you use the app might also seek permission to access your location when you're not using it*

Whatever type of permission you choose, after you make your decision, you might change your mind. For example, if you deny your location to an app, that app might lack some crucial functionality. Similarly, if you allow an app to use your location, you might have second thoughts about compromising your privacy.

Solution: Whatever the reason, you can control an app's access to your location by following these steps:

1. Open the Settings app.

2. Tap Privacy. The Privacy settings appear.

3. Tap Location Services. The Location Services screen appears.

4. Tap the app for which you want to configure access to GPS. The app's location access options appear. Figure 9-6 shows the options for the Foursquare app.

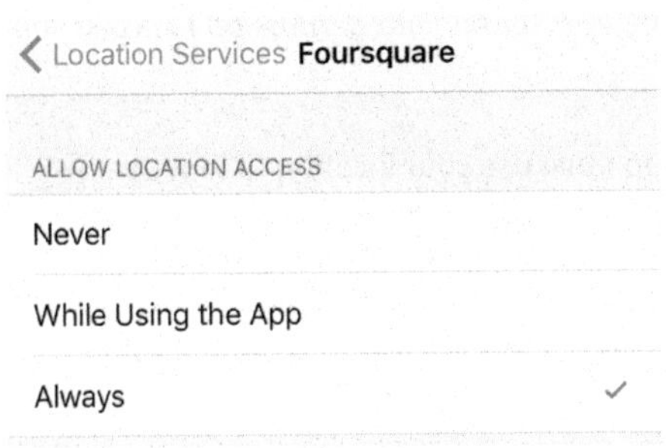

❮ Location Services **Foursquare**

ALLOW LOCATION ACCESS

Never

While Using the App

Always ✓

Figure 9-6. *Use these options to configure an app's access to your location*

5. Tap one of the following options to configure the app's access to your location:

- **Never**. Tap this option if you want to deny your current location to the app.

- **While Using the App**. Tap this option if you want to allow a specific app to access your current location only when you are actively using the app.

- **Always**. Tap this option if the app requires your location to function even when you're not using it. (Note that this option is only available for apps that require full-time access to GPS.)

You Want to Stop One or More System Services from Using Your Location

iOS also provides location services to various internal system services that perform tasks, such as calibrating the compass, setting the time zone, and serving up Apple Ads that change depending on location data. You might prefer that iOS not provide your location to one or more of these services.

Solution: If you don't want iOS providing your location to some of these services, you can prevent this by following these steps:

1. Open the Settings app.

2. Tap Privacy. The Privacy screen appears.

3. Tap Location Services. The Location Services screen appears.

4. Tap System Services. iOS displays the System Services screen. The iPhone version of this screen is shown in Figure 9-7.

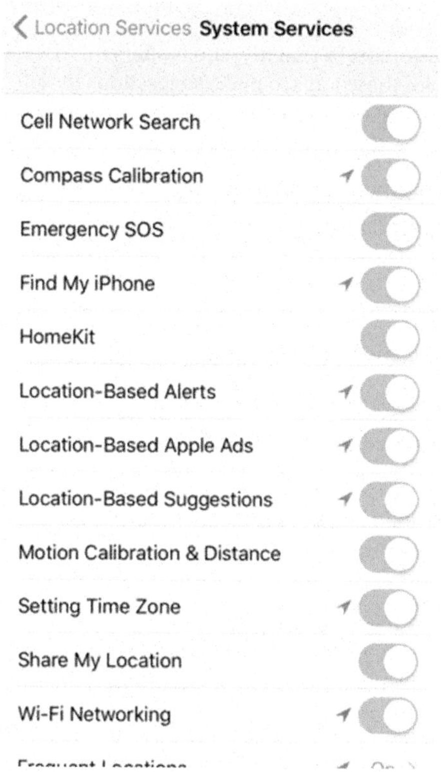

‹ Location Services **System Services**

Cell Network Search	
Compass Calibration	
Emergency SOS	
Find My iPhone	
HomeKit	
Location-Based Alerts	
Location-Based Apple Ads	
Location-Based Suggestions	
Motion Calibration & Distance	
Setting Time Zone	
Share My Location	
Wi-Fi Networking	

Figure 9-7. *Tap the switch to Off beside any system service that you want to deny access to your location*

5. For any system service to which you don't want to provide access to location data, tap its switch to Off.

Tip It's also important to know when a system service is using your location. To set this up, scroll to the bottom of the System Services screen and tap the Status Bar Icon switch to On. iOS will now use the status bar to display one of the icons shown above this switch whenever a system service is using your location.

You Want to Prevent iOS from Storing a List of Your Frequent Locations

iOS keeps track of the physical locations you visit most frequently, and it offers this data to apps such as Maps and Calendar. This enables these apps to make suggestions based on your location history, but you might prefer that iOS not keep track of your frequent locations for privacy reasons.

Solution: You can enhance your privacy not only by clearing the list of frequent locations, but also by preventing iOS from maintaining this list at all. Here are the steps to follow:

1. Open the Settings app.

2. Tap Privacy. The Privacy screen appears.

3. Tap Location Services. The Location Services screen appears.

4. Tap System Services. iOS displays the System Services screen.

5. Tap Frequent Locations to open the Frequent Locations screen.

6. To remove the current list of frequent locations, tap Clear History, and then when asked to confirm, tap Clear History once again.

7. To prevent iOS from storing your oft-used location, tap the Frequent Locations switch to Off, as shown in Figure 9-8.

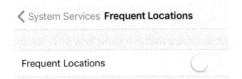

Figure 9-8. To prevent iOS from tracking your most-used locations, tap the Frequent Locations switch to Off

You Do Not Want to Share Your Location with your Family and Friends

When you set up Family Sharing on your iCloud account, one of the setup screens asks if you want to share your location with your family using the Messages and Find My Friends apps. If you initially decided to share your location, you might later decide to change your mind and keep your location private.

Solution: You can disable this feature by following these steps:

1. Open the Settings app.

2. Tap Privacy. The Privacy screen appears.

3. Tap Location Services. The Location Services screen appears.

4. Tap Share My Location to open the Share My Location screen.

5. Tap the Share My Location switch to Off, as shown in Figure 9-9.

Figure 9-9. *To no longer allow family and friends to see your location, tap the Share My Location switch to Off*

You Do Not Want Uour Device Usage Information Being Sent to Apple

iOS constantly monitors your device resources to watch out for adverse events. Then can include memory getting too low, processor usage getting too high, an app crashing, or the system spontaneously rebooting. When it detects such events, iOS records the current system state and writes this data to a diagnostics file. Figure 9-10 shows a typical entry.

❮ Data **stacks-2016-09-28-101648.ips**

{"bug_type":"288","timestamp":"2016-09-28 10:16:48.50
-0400","os_version":"iPhone OS 10.0.2
(14A456)","incident_id":"34E25C0E-11DB-4D14-8860-6E8AD3D485A9")
{
    "build" : "iPhone OS 10.0.2 (14A456)",
    "product" : "iPhone7,2",
    "kernel" : "Darwin Kernel Version 16.0.0: Sun Aug 28 20:36:55 PDT 2016;
root:xnu-3789.2.4~3\/RELEASE_ARM64_T7000",
    "tuning" : {

    },
    "incident" : "34E25C0E-11DB-4D14-8860-6E8AD3D485A9",
    "crashReporterKey" : "d979efab01fdfea47f705a4f39b2bbb8b7b3d3c0",
    "date" : "2016-09-28 10:16:48.50 -0400",
    "reason" : "sysdiagnose (post-spindump) stackshot",
    "frontmostPids" : [
        330,
        57
    ],
    "exception" : "0xbaaaaaad",
    "absoluteTime" : 818231903048,
    "memoryStatus" : {"compressorSize":42251,"compressions":
368778,"decompressions":170242,"busyBufferCount":9,"jetsamLevel":
0,"pageSize":4096,"memoryPressure":{"pagesWanted":
0,"pagesReclaimed":46818},"memoryPages":{"active":101307,"throttled":
0,"fileBacked":91765,"wired":52661,"purgeable":1540,"inactive":
46644,"free":4483,"speculative":5201}},
    "processByPid" : {
        "0" : {
        "timesThrottled" : 0,
        "pageIns" : 1,
        "timesDidThrottle" : 0,
        "dup_images" : [

        ],
        "procname" : "kernel_task",
        "copyOnWriteFaults" : 0,
        "threadById" : {
            "417" : {
            "continuation" : [
                0,
                68841758156
            ],
            "userTime" : 0.015846833,
            "systemTime" : 0,
            "id" : 417,
            "basePriority" : 81,
            "name" : "AppleSmartIO",
            "user_usec" : 15846,
            "schedPriority" : 81.

Figure 9-10. *A typical diagnostics entry*

As you can see, the data is for the most part highly technical. That's because it's meant to be used by Apple engineers when diagnosing a problem with your device or an app.

■ **Note**   To view your diagnostics and usage entries, open Settings, tap Privacy, tap Diagnostics and Usage, and then tap Diagnostics & Usage Data.

However, iOS also periodically creates diagnostic logs and sends them to Apple for analysis. These logs are useful to Apple for fixing bugs and improving their products, but they are anonymous and generally do not contain any personal data. I say "generally" here because Apple does include location data in these logs.

Despite this, you might feel uncomfortable sending your usage and diagnostics data to Apple, particularly your location.

Solution: You can prevent iOS from including your location in its diagnostic and usage logs by following these steps:

1. Open the Settings app.

2. Tap Privacy. The Privacy screen appears.

3. Tap Location Services. The Location Services screen appears.

4. Tap System Services. iOS displays the System Services screen.

5. Tap the Diagnostics & Usage switch to Off, as shown in Figure 9-11.

Figure 9-11. *To prevent iOS from sending your location along with its diagnostics logs, tap the Diagnostics & Usage switch to Off*

If you don't want iOS to send any diagnostics and usage logs to Apple, you can disable this feature by following these steps:

1. Open the Settings app.

2. Tap Privacy. The Privacy screen appears.

3. Tap Diagnostics & Usage. The Diagnostics & Usage screen appears.

4. Tap Don't Send, as shown in Figure 9-12.

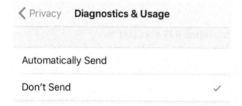

Figure 9-12. *To prevent iOS from sending any diagnostic and usage logs to Apple, display the Diagnostics & Usage screen and then tap Don't Send*

You Do Not Want to Receive Targeted Ads

In much the same way that online advertisers can track you across the Web using cookies (small text files that the advertisers store on your computer), app advertisers can track your interests using a piece of data called the Advertising Identifier. This is an anonymous device identifier that iOS uses when you perform certain actions, such as searching the App Store. Advertisers have access to the Advertising Identifier and can use it to serve you ads that are selected based on your usage. You might prefer not to receive these targeted ads.

Solution: You can configure your privacy settings to tell advertisers not to use the Advertising Identifier to track your interests and actions. You can also reset the Advertising Identifier value, which is similar to deleting the tracking cookies on your computer.

Follow these steps:

1. Open the Settings app.

2. Tap Privacy. The Privacy screen appears.

3. Tap Advertising. The Advertising screen appears.

4. Tap the Limit Add Tracking switch to On, as shown in Figure 9-13.

Figure 9-13. To prevent advertisers from using the Advertising Identifier to send you targeted ads, activate the Limit Ad Tracking setting

5. Tap Reset Advertising Identifier and, when iOS asks you to confirm, tap Reset Identifier.

Another way that iOS serves you targeted ads is via your location. Here are the steps to follow to turn off this privacy breach:

1. Open the Settings app.

2. Tap Privacy. The Privacy screen appears.

3. Tap Location Services. The Location Services screen appears.

4. Tap System Services. iOS displays the System Services screen.

5.   Tap the Location-Based Apple Ads switch to Off, as shown in
      Figure 9-14.

Figure 9-14. *Tap Location-Based Apple Ads to Off to prevent seeing targeted ads based on your location.*

You Do Not Want to Be Shown Apps That Are Popular in Your Area

The App Store uses your location to tell you which apps are the most popular near you. You might prefer not to be targeted in this way due to privacy concerns.

Solution: Follow these steps to turn off this tracking feature:

1.   Open the Settings app.

2.   Tap Privacy. The Privacy screen appears.

3.   Tap Location Services. The Location Services screen appears.

4.   Tap System Services. iOS displays the System Services screen.

5.   Tap the Popular Near Me switch to Off, as shown in Figure 9-15.

Figure 9-15. *To prevent iOS from using your location to determine popular nearby apps, tap the Popular Near Me switch to Off*

Troubleshooting Web Browsing Privacy Issues

The rest of this chapter takes you through a few troubleshooting techniques related to enhancing the privacy of your web browsing sessions.

You Want to Delete the List of Websites You've Visited

Safari's History list – the collection of sites you've recently surfed – is a great feature when you need it, and it's an innocuous feature when you don't. However, there are times when the History list is just plain uncool. For example, if you visit a private corporate site, a financial site, or any other site you wouldn't want others to see, the History list might betray you.

And sometimes unsavory sites can end up in your History list by accident. For example, you might tap a legitimate-looking link in a web page or email message, only to end up in some dark, unpleasant web neighborhood. Of course, you high-tail it out of there right away with a quick tap of the Back button, but that nasty site is now lurking in your history.

■ **Caution**   As of iOS 9, clearing your Safari history also clears your cookies and website data. Clearing cookies might present problems since many of them store site login data or site customizations. Therefore, when clearing your history, consider only clearing recent data (such as data from the previous hour).

Solution: Whether you've got sites on the History list that you wouldn't want anyone to see, or you just find the idea of Safari tracking your movements on the Web to be a bit sinister, follow these steps to wipe out the History list:

1. In Safari, tap the Bookmarks button. Safari opens the Bookmarks list.

2. Tap Back until you get to the Bookmarks screen.

3. Tap History. Safari opens the History screen.

4. Tap Clear. Safari asks how much of your history you want to clear, as shown in Figure 9-16.

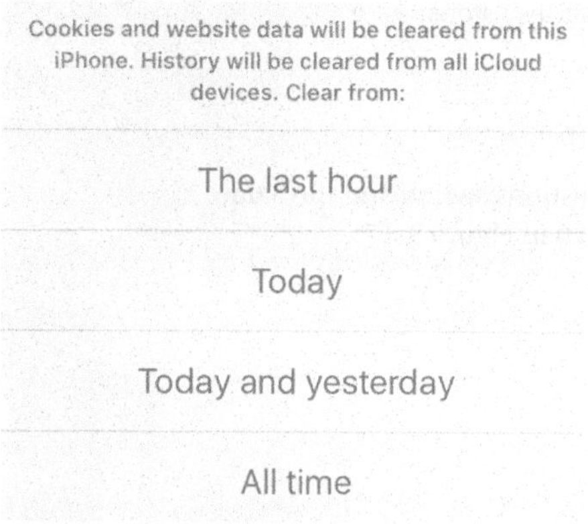

Cookies and website data will be cleared from this
iPhone. History will be cleared from all iCloud
devices. Clear from:

The last hour

Today

Today and yesterday

All time

Figure 9-16. *Tap Clear and then tap how much of your web browsing history you want to delete*

5. Tap a time period: The Last Hour, Today, Today and Yesterday, or All Time. Safari deletes every site from the History list for that time period.

■ **Note** Safari uses your history (as well as your bookmarks) to analyze each page you view and determine the most likely link you'll tap — the so-called *top hit* — and preloads that link. If you do tap that link, the page loads lickety-split. However, if you're not comfortable having Safari send your history and bookmarks to Apple, you can turn this feature off. Tap Settings, tap Safari, and then tap the Preload Top Hit switch to Off (see Figure 9-17).

You Do Not Want Safari to Show Suggestions When You Search

Another way Safari might compromise your online privacy is by displaying suggestions as you enter search text into the address bar. If someone is looking over your shoulder or simply borrows your device for a quick search, she might see these suggestions.

Solution: To turn these suggestions off, follow these steps:

1. Open the Settings app.

2. Tap Safari to open the Safari screen.

3. Tap both the Search Engine Suggestions switch and the Safari Suggestions switch to Off, as shown in Figure 9-17.

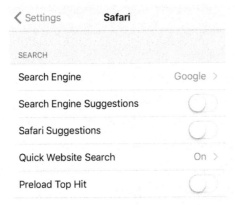

Figure 9-17. You can prevent Safari from making suggestions that other people might be able to see

You Want to Browse the Web without Storing Data About the Sites You Visit

If you find yourself constantly deleting your browsing history or website data, you can save yourself a bit of time by configuring Safari to do this automatically. This is called *private browsing* and it means that Safari doesn't save any data as you browse. Specifically, it doesn't save the following:

- Sites aren't added to the history (although the Back and Forward buttons still work for navigating sites that you've visited in the current session).

- Web page text and images aren't saved.

- Search text isn't saved with the search box.

- AutoFill passwords aren't saved.

Solution: To activate private browsing, follow these steps:

1. In Safari, tap the Tabs button.

2. Tap Private. Safari creates a separate set of tabs for private browsing.

3. Tap Add Tab (+). Safari creates a new private tab.

When you're done browsing privately, tap the Tabs icon and then tap the Private button to turn off Private Browsing.

You Want to Ensure You're Not Being Tracked by Online Advertisers

Under the guise of providing you with the "benefit" of targeted ads, online advertisers use cookies to track the websites you visit, the searches you conduct, and so on. This data isn't linked to you personally, but no one likes to be tracked in this way. Fortunately, iOS Safari is configured by default to minimize this kind of tracking, but you might want to confirm – or even strengthen – these settings.

Solution: Preventing online tracking involves two things. First, make sure Safari's Do Not Track setting is activated, which tells advertisers not to track you online. Note, however, that it does not force advertisers not to track you. Compliance is voluntary, but you should activate the setting anyway for the few advertisers who do honor it.

Second, you need to decide the level at which you want to block cookies. You have four choices:

- **Always Block.** This level tells Safari not to accept any cookies. I don't recommend this level because it disables functionality on many websites (for example, a site's ability to save your login data and customizations).

- **Allow from Current Website Only.** This level tells Safari to only accept cookies that are set by whatever website you are currently visiting. No other website – in particular, no online advertising site – can set a cookie. If you want to strengthen Safari's ad-blocking, this is the setting to use, although there's a chance you might lose some functionality (see the next item).

- **Allow from Websites I Visit.** This level tells Safari to only accept cookies not only from the current website, but also from any website you've visited in the past. For example, suppose you have earlier visited the YouTube site. If the current site wants to set a YouTube cookie, then this setting will allow it. If you've never visited a site in the past – which will be the case for the vast majority of online advertising sites – then Safari blocks cookies from that site. This is the default setting, and it's a good compromise because sites you've previously visited might need to access a cookie to implement some functionality on your current site (such as account data).

- **Always Allow.** This level tells Safari to accept any cookie from any site. Avoid this setting because it means that any online advertiser who does not honor the Do Not Track setting (which is, alas, the vast majority of them) will use cookies to track you.

Follow these steps to configure Safari to ensure you're not being tracked by online advertisers:

1. Open the Settings app.

2. Tap Safari to open the Safari screen.

3. If needed, tap the Do Not Track switch to On.

4. Tap Block Cookies to open the Block Cookies screen, shown in Figure 9-18.

Figure 9-18. *Safari's cookie-blocking settings*

5. Tap the cookie-blocking setting you prefer to use.

You Want to Remove Your Saved Credit Card Data

In Chapter 4, "Resolving Web Issues," you learned how to save time and effort by storing your credit card data inside Safari. That's convenient, but it's also dangerous if you lend your device or if someone obtain your device while it's unlocked.

Solution: You can follow these steps to remove a saved credit card:

1. Open the Settings app.

2. Tap Safari to open the Safari screen.

3. Tap AutoFill to open the AutoFill screen.

4. Tap Saved Credit Cards. iOS prompts you to enter your passcode or Touch ID, if either is set up.

5. Type your passcode or apply your fingerprint to open the Credit Cards screen.

6. Tap Edit.

7. Tap the credit card you want to remove, then tap Delete.

You Want to Remove Your Saved Website Passwords

You can configure Safari's AutoFill feature to save website usernames and passwords. That's a real convenience, but it means that anyone who has access to your unlocked device will be able to log in to any of those sites.

Solution: To avoid this problem, you can delete one or more of your saved website passwords. Here are the steps to follow:

1. Open the Settings app.

2. Tap Safari to open the Safari screen.

3. Tap Passwords. iOS prompts you to enter your passcode or Touch ID, if either is set up.

4. Type your passcode or apply your fingerprint to open the Passwords screen.

5. Tap Edit.

6. Tap each password you want to remove, then tap Delete.

■ ■ ■

CHAPTER 10

Repairing Battery and Charging Problems

One of the oddities of the modern digital world is that while our devices have undergone mind-blowing increases in performance, miniaturization, and overall technical sophistication over the past decade or so, the battery life of those devices has increased comparatively slowly. For example, from the iPhone 4s to the iPhone 6 – four generations – battery life for using the Internet over Wi-Fi increased from 9 hours to 11 hours. Apple claims the iPhone 7 Plus will get 15 hours, but even a 67 percent increase over six generations is nothing to brag about. Given the importance we place on our iOS devices, it's no wonder that the number one gripe by far among users is poor battery life and the number one request by far for each new generation is better – *much* better – battery performance. Unfortunately, there are many technical reasons why we won't see a radical increase in battery life for our iOS devices any time soon. That means we need to take steps now to monitor and maximize the batteries that we have.

Tracking Battery Use

iOS doesn't give a ton of battery data, but you can monitor both the total usage time (this includes all activities: calling, surfing, playing media, and so on) and standby time (time when your iOS device was in sleep mode). Also, one of the nice features in iOS is a breakdown of recent (the last three hours) battery usage by app, so you can see which apps have been draining your battery.

You Want to Know Exactly How Much Battery Power You Have Left

By default, iOS displays a battery icon in the status bar (see Figure 10-1). As the battery drains, the amount of white inside the icon gets smaller, and the level turns red when the amount of battery power gets low enough that you need to start paying attention. This is useful information, to be sure, but it's all a bit vague and imprecise.

© Paul McFedries 2017
P. McFedries, *Troubleshooting iOS*, DOI 10.1007/978-1-4842-2445-8_10

Figure 10-1. *The iOS battery icon appears in the status bar*

Solution: To keep closer tabs on your device battery life, you need to tell iOS to also display the percentage of battery power remaining. Here are the steps to follow:

1. On the Home screen, tap Settings to open the Settings app.

2. Tap Battery to open the Battery screen.

3. Tap the Battery Percentage switch to On, as shown in Figure 10-2.

Figure 10-2. *Tap the Battery Percentage switch to On to add the percentage of battery power remaining to the status bar icon*

You Want to Know How Much You're Using Your Device on Battery Power

Apple puts out lots of battery life numbers that include both usage mode (that is, when your device is on) and standby mode (when your device is asleep). But if you need to know whether your device will have enough battery power for, say, a long plane ride or some similar extended time away from a power outlet, can you really trust Apple numbers?

Solution: Fortunately, you don't have to trust Apple on this because iOS keeps track of your devices overall battery use. Specifically, it tracks the amount of time since the last full charge that your device has been in usage mode and in standby mode. By tracking these numbers over time and over several charging cycles, you'll get to know how much battery life your iOS device gets when you use it.

Follow these steps to view these numbers:

1. On the Home screen, tap Settings to open the Settings app.

2. Tap Battery to open the Battery screen.

3. Scroll to the bottom of the screen and read the Usage and Standby values, as shown in Figure 10-3.

TIME SINCE LAST FULL CHARGE	
Usage	1 hr, 16 min
Standby	6 hr, 21 min

Figure 10-3. *Scroll to the bottom of the Battery screen to read the total time since the last full charge that your iOS device has been in usage and standby modes*

You Suspect an App Has Been Using Too Much Battery Power

One of the benefits of adding the percentage value to the status bar's battery icon and monitoring the Usage time in the Battery screen of the Settings app is that you get to know how your apps use battery power. In particular, you might notice that your battery seems to drain a little faster than normal when you use a particular app. That's useful to know, but how can you be sure?

Solution: iOS can help by breaking down your device's battery usage by app. For both the last 24 hours and the last 7 days, you see the percentage of total battery power that each app has used. You can also display the total amount of time each app has used the battery both when the app was onscreen and when it was running in the background.

If you see that a particular app has been using far more battery life than you think it should – particularly if you don't use the app much more than your other apps – it might indicate a problem. For example, the app might have a memory leak, or it might be running tasks in the background.

Follow these steps to view battery usage by app:

1. On the Home screen, tap Settings to open the Settings app.

2. Tap Battery to open the Battery screen.

3. In the Battery Usage section (see Figure 10-4), tap to switch between seeing usage for the Last 24 Hours and the Last 7 Days.

4.   Tap the Time icon (pointed out in Figure 10-4) to toggle the total onscreen and background usage times for each app.

Figure 10-4. *In the Battery screen, the Battery Usage section breaks down battery percentage and, optionally, battery usage times, by app*

Extending Battery Life

Reducing battery consumption as much as possible on your iOS device not only extends the time between charges but also extends the overall life of your battery. The Battery Usage screen usually offers a suggestion or two for extending battery life, but there are many other steps you can take.

You Want to Prevent All Your Apps from Running in the Background

One of the best battery usage tools that iOS has to offer is the Time icon in the Battery screen (see Figure 10-4, earlier). When activated, this feature tells you not only how much time each app has been using the battery while onscreen but, more importantly, how much time each app has been draining battery power in the background. The capability of an app to perform tasks in the background is called Background App Refresh and it's important because although you know when an app is active onscreen, you don't always know when it's active in the background, since iOS usually gives you no indication.

In practical terms, this means that if your battery is running low, you can stop using certain apps, but you won't know if those or other apps are still working – and therefore using up precious battery power – in the background.

Solution: You can deactivate Background App Refresh for all apps by following these steps:

1. On the Home screen, tap Settings to open the Settings app.

2. Tap General to open the General screen.

3. Tap Background App Refresh to open the Background App Refresh screen.

4. Tap the Background App Refresh switch to Off, as shown in Figure 10-5).

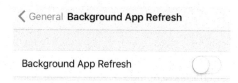

Figure 10-5. *When faced with a low battery, turn off Background App Refresh to prevent any app from running in the background*

You Want to Prevent a Specific App from Running in the Background

By regularly examining the battery usage of your apps – both as an overall percentage and as total time onscreen and in the background – you will eventually come to recognize any battery hogs. In particular, you'll come to know which apps are using up your device battery by running background tasks. Turning off Background App Refresh for all apps seems like overkill in this case, particularly if it's just a single app that's causing a problem.

Solution: If you see that a particular app is using up a higher than average amount of battery power in background tasks, and if you don't feel it's necessary for the app to run in the background, you can deactivate Background App Refresh for just that app.
Here are the steps to follow:

1. On the Home screen, tap Settings to open the Settings app.

2. Tap General to open the General screen.

3. Tap Background App Refresh to open the Background App Refresh screen.

4. In the list of apps, tap the switch to Off beside the app you no longer want to operate in the background, as shown in Figure 10-6.

Figure 10-6. *You can disable Background App Refresh for an individual app that's been using up too much battery power while running in the background*

You Want Your iOS Device to Use Less Battery Power

When your iOS device battery is running low, or if you still have plenty of battery power but you know you'll need to use the device for a long stretch, it would be advantageous to configure the device to use less battery power on other tasks.

Solution: You learn quite a few techniques for preserving battery power in the next section. However, iOS offers an easy method for reducing the overall power consumption of your device. It's called Low Power Mode and it saves battery life by doing the following:

- Turning off Background App Refresh

- Disabling the Mail app's push feature (where the app checks for new mail automatically)

- Deactivating all automatic content downloads

- Preventing all automatic app upgrade

- Disabling a few visual effects

- Dimming the screen

iOS asks if you want to switch to Lower Power mode when the battery level falls to 20 percent, as shown in Figure 10-7. (This message appears again when the level falls to 10 percent.) Tap Low Power Mode to activate this feature.

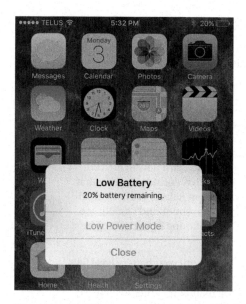

Figure 10-7. *When your device's battery level falls to 20 percent, iOS asks if you want to switch to Low Power Mode*

To activate Low Power Mode manually, follow these steps:

1. On the Home screen, tap Settings to open the Settings app.

2. Tap Battery to open the Battery screen.

3. Tap the Low Power Mode switch to On, as shown in Figure 10-8. Note that you can tell when this feature is active by looking at the battery icon, which turns yellow during Low Power Mode.

■ **Note**   With Low Power mode on, iOS automatically configures your device to auto-lock in 30 seconds and it disables the Auto-Lock setting.

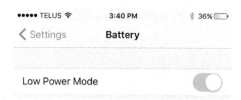

Figure 10-8. *To activate Low Power Mode manually, open the Battery screen in the Settings app and then tap the Low Power Mode switch to On*

You Want to Use as Little Battery Power as Possible

If battery power is scarce, there's no power outlet in sight, but you really need to use your iOS device, then you need to minimize the amount of battery power the device uses.

Solution: Here are a few suggestions to try that should help you to reduce your device's battery consumption to a minimal, while still retaining some functionality:

- **Deactivate Background App Refresh.** When you're desperate for juice, you probably don't need your apps working in the background. See the section "You want to prevent all your apps from running in the background," to learn how to turn off Background App Refresh. As an alternative, consider leaving that switch on but turning off Background App Refresh for individual apps (particularly active apps such as Facebook and Gmail); see the section "You want to prevent a specific app from running in the background."

- **Turn on Low Power Mode.** Don't wait until your battery level falls to 20 percent, which is when iOS automatically offers to turn on Low Power Mode for you. Turn it on manually earlier to increase battery life. I showed you how to activate Low Power Mode by hand in the section "You want your iOS device to use less battery power."

- **Dim the screen.** The touchscreen drains a lot of battery power, so dimming it reduces the amount of power used. On the Home screen, tap Settings, tap Display & Brightness, and then drag the Brightness slider to the left to dim the screen. Also, tap the Auto-Brightness switch to Off, as shown in Figure 10-9.

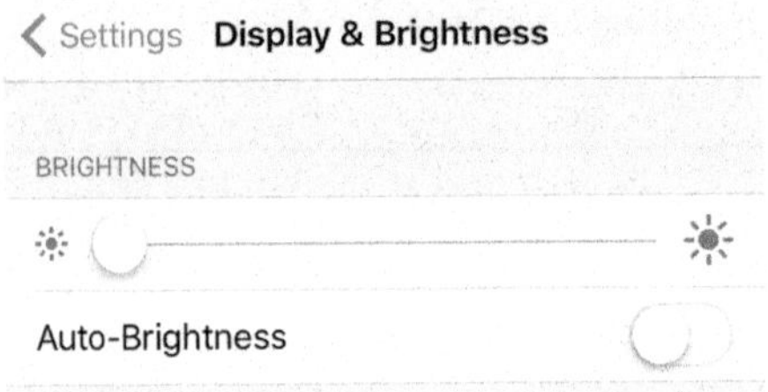

Figure 10-9. Dim the screen to the lowest brightness that lets you still read the screen, and turn off the Auto-Brightness feature

- **Slow the auto-check on your email.** Having your email frequently poll the server for new messages eats up your battery. Set it to check every hour or, ideally, set it to Manual check if you can. To do this, tap Settings, tap Mail, tap Accounts, and then tap Fetch New Data. In the Fetch section, tap either Hourly or Manually.

- **Turn off push.** If you're not using Low Power Mode and if you have an iCloud or Exchange account, consider turning off the push feature to save battery power. Tap Settings, tap Mail, tap Accounts, and then tap Fetch New Data. In the Fetch New Data screen, tap the Push switch to Off, and in the Fetch section, tap Manually. See Figure 10-10.

Figure 10-10. Turn off Push to ensure that this background task doesn't eat up your battery

- **Minimize the number of apps you run.** If you won't be able to charge your iOS device for a while, avoid background chores, such as playing music; or secondary chores, such as organizing your contacts. If your only goal is to read all your email, stick to that until it's done because you don't know how much time you have.

- **Make sure Auto-Lock is working.** You don't want your iOS device using up battery power while it's idle, so make sure Auto-Lock is on the job. Open Settings, tap Display & Brightness, tap Auto-Lock, and then tap a short time interval (such as 1 Minute on the iPhone or 2 Minutes on the iPad).

- **Put your iOS device into sleep mode manually, if necessary.** If you are interrupted – for example, the pizza delivery guy shows up on time – don't wait for your iOS device to put itself to sleep because those few seconds or minutes use precious battery time. Instead, put your device to sleep manually right away by pressing the Sleep/Wake button.

- **Turn off Wi-Fi if you don't need it.** When Wi-Fi is on, it regularly checks for available wireless networks, which drains the battery. If you don't need to connect to a wireless network, turn off Wi-Fi to conserve energy. Open Settings, tap Wi-Fi, and then tap the Wi-Fi switch to Off.

- **Turn off cellular data if you don't need it.** Your iPhone or cellular-enabled iPad constantly looks for nearby cellular towers to maintain the signal, which can use up battery power in a hurry. If you're surfing on a Wi-Fi network, you don't need cellular data, so turn it off. Open Settings, tap Cellular, and then tap the Cellular Data switch to Off.

- **Turn off GPS if you don't need it.** When GPS is on, the receiver exchanges data with the GPS system regularly, which uses up battery power. If you don't need the GPS feature for the time being, turn off the GPS antenna. Open Settings, tap Privacy, tap Location Services, and then tap the Location Services switch to Off.

- **Turn off Bluetooth if you don't need it.** When Bluetooth is running, it constantly checks for nearby Bluetooth devices, and this drains the battery. If you aren't using any Bluetooth devices, turn off Bluetooth to save energy. Open Settings, tap Bluetooth, and then tap the Bluetooth switch to Off.

■ **Note** If you don't need all four of the device antennae — Wi-Fi, cellular, GPS, and Bluetooth — for a while, a faster way to turn them off is to switch your iOS device to airplane mode. Either open Settings and then tap the Airplane Mode switch to On, or swipe up from the bottom to reveal the Control Center and then tap the Airplane Mode icon.

Troubleshooting Other Battery Problems

I'll close this chapter with a quick look at two more solutions to battery-related problems.

You Want to Maximize your Battery's Lifespan

It's important to maximize battery life on days when you don't have nearby power, but it's also important to ensure that you maximize your battery's entire lifespan.

Solution: The lithium-ion (li-on) battery in your iOS device is much more forgiving than older battery technologies such as nickel-cadmium (NiCad). With just a few simple techniques and precautions, you can ensure that your battery gives good performance throughout the life of your iOS device:

- **Minimize the number of cycles the battery has to charge.** Your iOS device battery is designed to maintain up to 80 percent of its original capacity after 500 complete discharge and charge cycles. Discharging down to zero percent and recharging counts as one cycle, discharging to 50 percent and recharging counts as half a cycle, and so on. Your iOS device will reach that 500-cycle mark slower if you plug it into a power source as often as it's convenient.

- **Use the battery.** Don't think, however, that you'll keep the battery pristine by never using it. Li-on batteries require regular use or they'll refuse to charge.

- **Don't cycle the battery.** *Cycling* – also called reconditioning or recalibrating – a battery means letting it completely discharge and then fully recharging it again. This was important in earlier battery technologies, but not with the Li-on battery in your iOS device. Letting the battery percentage drop to around 50 percent before recharging seems to be the sweet spot for maximizing battery life.

- **Avoid temperature extremes.** Exposing your iOS device to extremely hot or cold temperatures reduces the long-term effectiveness of the battery. Try to keep your iOS device at a reasonable temperature.

- **Try not to drop your iOS device.** Dropping the device can damage the battery, resulting in poor battery performance or even eventual failure.

- **Use a high-quality charger.** Cheap chargers can damage batteries beyond repair. Either use the charger that came with your iOS device, or use a third-party charger that was designed to work with your specific make and model of iOS device.

- **Don't store your iOS device at full charge.** If you won't be using your iOS device for a few weeks, or even longer, you'll likely be tempted to give it a full charge before putting it in storage. However, for longer life, it's better to store the device with the battery partially discharged – to, say, between 40 and 60 percent.

■ **Caution**   It's even more important not to store your iOS device with its battery fully discharged. This can damage the battery to the point where it won't charge at all when you plug the device back in.

Your Battery Won't Charge

When you plug your iOS device into a power outlet, you might find that it does not charge.

Solution: If you find that your battery won't charge, here are some possible solutions:

- If the iOS device is plugged in to a computer to charge via the USB port, it may be that the computer has gone into standby. Waking the computer should solve the problem.

- The USB port might not be transferring enough power. For example, the USB ports on most keyboards and hubs don't offer much in the way of power. If you have your iOS device plugged in to a USB port on a keyboard or hub, plug it in to a USB port on your Mac or PC.

- Attach the USB cable to the USB power adapter, and then plug the adapter in to a power outlet.

- Double-check all connections to make sure everything is plugged in properly.

- Try another Lightning cable if you have one.

- If the iOS device hasn't been charged in a long time, its battery might have gone into sleep mode to protect itself from long-term damage. In this case, it will take a few minutes – perhaps as long as ten minutes – before the battery wakes up and starts charging in the normal manner.

If none of these suggestions solves the problem, you may need to send your iOS device in for service.

■ ■ ■

CHAPTER 11

Getting Around Accessibility Issues

The promise of an iPhone, iPad, or iPod touch is information at your fingertips. But what if mobility challenges make it difficult to control your hands, much less your fingertips? What if visual challenges make it hard to even see the information? Whether you've had to overcome physical disabilities since you were young or you're discovering new physical limitations almost daily as you get older, that doesn't mean you have to be shut out of the digital device revolution. True, iOS devices can be difficult or impossible to use if you have visual, aural, or physical challenges. But that's only because the default settings seem to have been chosen to benefit twenty-somethings in perfect health. The good news is that you don't have to settle for these defaults. iOS is chock full of useful settings, options, and techniques that can turn any device from being a pain (literally, in some cases) to use, to a pleasure (at least relatively speaking). In this chapter, I take you through various problems related to using an iOS device while dealing with visual, hearing, and physical limitations, and you learn how to configure iOS to enable you to work around those limitations and get the most out of your device.

Working Around Visual Challenges

Those of you who are no longer spring chickens (or even summer chickens, for that matter) know one thing for certain: the older you get, the worse your eyesight becomes. Sure, you can ramp up your eyeglass prescription or invest in extra-strength reading glasses, but even that may not be enough when it comes to reading text and deciphering icons on your iOS device screen. And, of course, if your eyesight problems go beyond simple afflictions such as farsightedness or astigmatism, then a change of eyewear isn't going to help you make sense of what's happening on your screen.

Whatever the source of your visual challenges, you can't work with iOS if you can't see what iOS is trying to show you onscreen. Fortunately, you can put iOS to work, making it easier to see text, icons, and images. As you learn in this section, iOS offers a number of tools for enlarging screen items, making things easier to see, reducing visual distractions, and even hearing audio translations of what's on the screen.

© Paul McFedries 2017
P. McFedries, *Troubleshooting iOS*, DOI 10.1007/978-1-4842-2445-8_11

You Want to Make Text Easier to Read

If your [20/20] vision is available only in hindsight, you may be asking yourself a simple question: Why does everything on my device screen look so tiny? The icons are miniature, the buttons are minute, and the text is miniscule.

Solution: I'm happy to report that these things are not set in stone (electronically speaking). iOS offers several settings that can enlarge what you see on your screen, or make it clearer. Follow these steps to modify some or all of these settings:

1. On the Home screen, tap Settings to open the Settings app.

2. Tap General to display the General screen.

3. Tap Accessibility to display the Accessibility screen.

4. Tap Display Accommodations and then tap Reduce White Point to On to make whites less intense.

5. Tap Larger Text, then use the slider to set the text size you'd prefer (see Figure 11-1). You can also tap the Larger Accessibility Sizes switch to On to take advantage of apps that support a feature called Dynamic Type, which enables the apps to resize text according to the slider value you set.

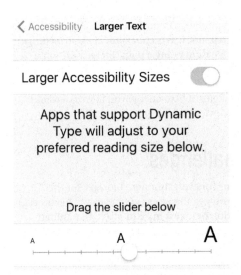

Figure 11-1. *You can use the Larger Text settings to increase the text size used by iOS and some apps*

6. Tap Bold Text to On to render all screen text in an easier-to-see bold font.

Note iOS requires you to restart your device to put the Bold Text setting into effect.

---

7. Tap Button Shapes to On to apply a fill color to all buttons (for example, see the General button in Figure 11-2), which make them easier to see and tap.

Figure 11-2. *Activate the Button Shapes setting to apply a fill that shows the shape of buttons, such as the General button shown here*

8. Tap Increase Contrast to improve overall screen contrast. Tap Reduce Transparency On to minimize transparency and blur effects; tap Darken Colors on to make non-white colors darker.

9. Tap Reduce Motion and then tap the Reduce Motion switch to On to tell iOS to use fewer user interface motion effects, which can make it easier to follow what's happening onscreen.

10. Tap the On/Off Labels switch to On to supplement each On/Off switch with a 1 that appears when the switch is on, or a 0 that appears when the switch is Off, as shown in Figure 11-3. This is useful if you have trouble distinguishing between the On and Off states of an iOS switch.

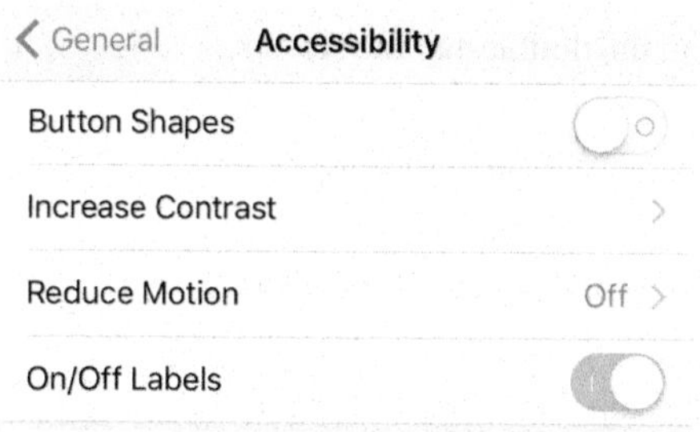

‹ General	Accessibility	
Button Shapes		◯
Increase Contrast		›
Reduce Motion	Off	›
On/Off Labels		

Figure 11-3. *When the On/Off Labels setting is activated, you see a 1 in a switch that's set to On, and a 0 in a switch that's set to Off*

You Want a Quick Way to Zoom in on the Screen

You may find that although you can make out most of the items on the screen, the occasional icon or bit of text is just too diminutive to decipher. Some of the settings mentioned in the previous section might help, but they affect all of iOS, which might be overkill.

Solution: You could always grab a nearby magnifying glass to get a closer look at the section you can't make out, but iOS offers an electronic version of the same thing. It's called Zoom, and it enables you to see a magnified portion of the screen. Here's how you enable it:

1. On the Home screen, tap Settings to open the Settings app.

2. Tap General to display the General screen.

3. Tap Accessibility to display the Accessibility screen.

4. Tap Zoom to display the Zoom screen.

5. Tap the Zoom switch to On, as shown in Figure 11-4. iOS adds the Zoom window, within which the underlying screen text and elements are magnified.

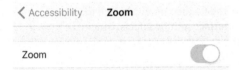

Figure 11-4. *Tap the Zoom switch to On to see the Zoom window, which magnifies a portion of the screen*

Here are some pointers for using the Zoom window:

•   To toggle the Zoom window off and on, double-tap the screen with three fingers.

•   To move the Zoom window, drag the oval handle that appears in the middle of its bottom border.

•   To move the screen within the Zoom window, drag three fingers inside the window.

•   To adjust the magnification, double-tap the screen with three fingers and then drag on the screen with three fingers.

•   To zoom the entire screen instead of just a portion of it, return to the Accessibility settings, tap Zoom, tap Zoom Region, and then tap Full Screen Zoom.

■ **Note** By default, Zoom automatically magnifies that portion of the screen that has the focus (that is, the portion of the screen with whatever control you're currently working with). If you find this jarring, you can disable it by displaying the Zoom screen and tapping the Follow Focus switch to Off.

You Want to Hear What's Shown on the Screen

If you find that you're really having trouble making out what's on the screen, you might prefer to have the screen text read to you.

Solution: iOS comes with an assistive technology called VoiceOver that can help. VoiceOver's job is to read aloud whatever text appears in the current screen or dialog. VoiceOver also does many other things, including the following:

- Tells you the name of the current app, as well as the name of the app's current screen or dialog.

- Tells you the name of the control that currently has the focus, the type of control (for example, a switch), and the control's current state (for example, On).

- Echoes your most recent keystroke. For example, if you press Delete to delete a character, VoiceOver says "Delete."

- Tells you the text of the current item, such as a text message.

Follow these steps to activate VoiceOver:

1. On the Home screen, tap Settings to open the Settings app.

2. Tap General to display the General screen.

3. Tap Accessibility to display the Accessibility screen.

4. Tap VoiceOver to display the VoiceOver screen.

5. Tap the VoiceOver switch to On, as shown in Figure 11-5. VoiceOver describes the current screen, including the alert button that Settings displays to ask you to confirm.

6. Tap OK twice.

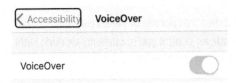

Figure 11-5. Tap the VoiceOver switch to On to hear what's displayed on the screen

---

▪ **Note**   VoiceOver overs an extensive collection of customization settings that enable you to control how verbose VoiceOver is; whether you want to hear sound effects; whether you want to hear characters, words, or both when typing; and more. You'll find all these settings on the VoiceOver screen.

Note that activating VoiceOver changes how you use the iOS interface as follows:

- Tap a screen item to select it and have VoiceOver tell you its name and optionally its state or text. iOS places a black border around the item to show you that it's selected. For an example, see the Accessibility button in Figure 11-5.

- To run, activate, or choose a screen item that you've already selected, double-tap it.

- To scroll, slide three fingers on the screen.

You Want to Use your iOS Device to Magnify Real-World Items

The Camera app comes with a zoom feature that, by spreading your fingers on the screen, lets you see a magnified version of the current frame. Besides being a useful photography feature, the zoom is handy for getting a closer look at items in the real world, such as tiny text or far-off signs. Unfortunately, the spread gesture isn't easy to use if you also have mobility challenges.

Solution: iOS offers a Magnifier tool that automatically launches the Camera app and activates its zoom feature. Here are the steps to follow to enable Magnifier:

1. On the Home screen, tap Settings to open the Settings app.

2. Tap General to display the General screen.

3. Tap Accessibility to display the Accessibility screen.

4. Tap Magnifier to display the Magnifier screen.

5. Tap the Magnifier switch to On, as shown in Figure 11-6.

■ **Tip**   If you find the zoomed screen too dark or too light at times, you can configure iOS to adjust automatically. In the Magnifier screen, tap the Auto-Brightness switch to On.

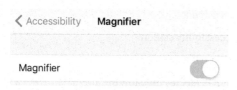

Figure 11-6. Tap the Magnifier switch to On to easily use the Camera app's zoom feature to get a closer look at real-world items

With Magnifier activated, you invoke it by triple-pressing the Home button.

Overcoming Physical Challenges

Using your iOS device may seem at first blush to be more of a mental exercise. After all, you spend lots of time in front of the screen reading things, looking at things, and thinking about things.

However, if you mapped out your device time, you'd almost certainly find that you spend great chunks of time on physical tasks: typing, tapping, double-tapping, and all the gestures – swiping, sliding, pinching, spreading, and so on – that are needed to make your device do your bidding.

This surprisingly physical side of iOS means that if you have physical challenges of your own, you may find it hard to perform certain tasks (and a few may be pretty much impossible). Fortunately, it doesn't have to be that way. iOS has quite a few settings and tools that either make using your device less of a burden or that enable you to work around any problems you might encounter.

Double-Clicking the Home Button Doesn't Display the Multitasking Screen

You switch between apps in iOS by double-clicking the Home button to open the multitasking screen, swiping until the app you want to switch to comes into view, and then tapping the app. Switching between apps is much more difficult if you can't access the multitasking screen.

Solution: If double-clicking the Home button doesn't display the multitasking screen, you might be taking too long between each press, so try a faster double-click.

If that's a persistent problem for you, you can slow down the Home-click speed. Here are the steps to follow:

1.   On the Home screen, tap Settings to open the Settings app.

2.   Tap General to display the General screen.

3.   Tap Accessibility to display the Accessibility screen.

4.   Tap Home Button to display the Home Button screen.

5.   Tap Slow, as shown in Figure 11-7. iOS flashes the Slow option and vibrates the device at the new Home-click speed.

6.   If you find that speed still causes problems, try using the Slowest speed, instead.

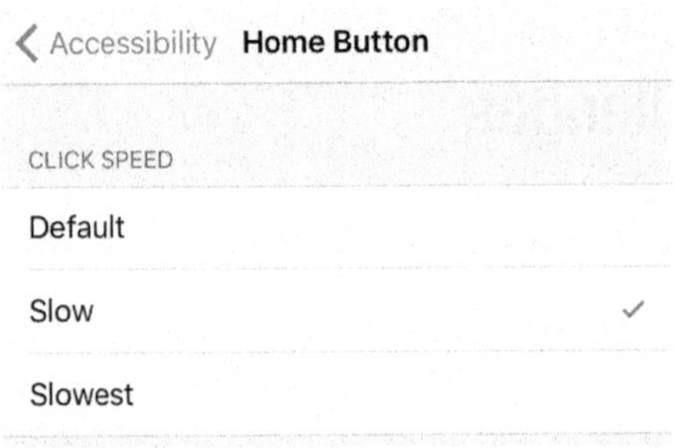

⟨ Accessibility   **Home Button**

CLICK SPEED

Default

Slow   ✓

Slowest

Figure 11-7.   If you're having trouble getting iOS to recognize Home button double-clicks, try the Slow speed

■ **Tip**   Once you get your Home button clicking problem solved, you can make your favorite accessibility tool easier to use by configuring iOS to launch it when you *triple*-click the Home button. Open Settings, tap General, tap Accessibility, and then tap Accessibility Shortcut (it's at the bottom of the screen). Tap one of the assistive technologies — such as VoiceOver or Zoom — in the list that appears. You can now invoke that tool by triple-clicking Home.

You Find It Difficult to Unlock Your Device Using Touch ID

You learned in Chapter 8, "Protecting Your Device," that you can use Touch ID to unlock your iOS device (see "You Want to Unlock Your Device with Your Fingerprint"). In iOS 9 and earlier, you unlocked the device by resting a digit with a saved fingerprint on the Home button. In iOS 10, however, you now have to press the Home button with that finger. You might find that a physical limitation makes it difficult to perform this technique.

Solution: You can tell iOS to allow a finger resting on the Home button to unlock your device. Here are the steps to follow:

1. On the Home screen, tap Settings to open the Settings app.

2. Tap General to display the General screen.

3. Tap Accessibility to display the Accessibility screen.

4. Scroll down and tap Home Button to display the Home Button screen.

5. Tap the Rest Finger to Open switch to On, as shown in Figure 11-8.

Figure 11-8. *Tap Rest Finger to Open to return to unlocking your iOS device just by resting a Touch ID finger on the Home button*

You're Getting Unwanted Keystrokes When You Type

If you want to enter a key multiple times, you can tap the key as many times as you need. However, when you press and hold a key, iOS assumes you want to enter that key multiple times. iOS first accepts the initial keystroke and then waits briefly (about half a second) to see whether you leave the key held down. If you do, iOS accepts multiple versions of the key until you release it.

These are useful techniques if, say, you're using the arrow keys to navigate a document or the Backspace key to delete a number of characters. They're decidedly not useful if you have mobility challenges that cause you to frequently bounce your finger on a key or hold down a key that you meant to press only once.

151

Solution: If you tend to press keys multiple times or hold keys down too long, the Key Repeat feature lets you filter out the extra characters that appear in these situations.

To use this feature, follow these steps to activate and configure it:

1. On the Home screen, tap Settings to open the Settings app.

2. Tap General to display the General screen.

3. Tap Accessibility to display the Accessibility screen.

4. Tap Keyboard to display the Keyboard screen.

5. Tap Key Repeat to display the Key Repeat screen.

6. If you don't want iOS to repeat characters when you press and hold a key, tap the Key Repeat switch to Off. Otherwise, tap this switch to On, as shown in Figure 11-9.

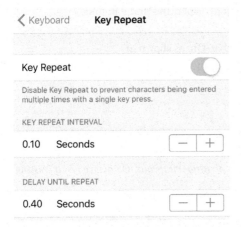

Figure 11-9. Tap Key Repeat Finger to Open to return to unlocking your iOS device just by resting a Touch ID finger on the Home button

7. If Key Repeat is On, use the Key Repeat Interval setting to set the amount of time that iOS waits between repeated keystrokes.

8. If Key Repeat is On, use the Delay Until Repeat setting to set the amount of time that iOS waits after the initial keystroke to begin repeating the keystroke.

iOS Sometimes Misinterprets or Does Not Recognize Your Taps

The touchscreen on your iOS device is a marvel of modern electronics: sensitive, versatile, and powerful. It's hard to imagine using iOS without it, so perhaps that's why touchscreen problems are so frustrating. If you find it difficult to control your hands, or if your dexterity isn't what it used to be, then you might run up against one or more of the following touchscreen troubles:

- If you tend to keep your tapping finger on the screen a bit too long, iOS interprets the gesture as a tap-and-hold rather than a simple tap.

- If you tend to bounce your tapping finger on the screen, iOS interprets the gesture as multiple taps rather than a single tap.

- If you tend to move your tapping finger along the screen, iOS interprets the gesture as a slide or swipe rather than a tap.

Solution: iOS comes with several so-called *touch accommodations* that you can activate and adjust as needed to get your taps recognized and/or interpreted correctly. Follow these steps:

1. On the Home screen, tap Settings to open the Settings app.

2. Tap General to display the General screen.

3. Tap Accessibility to display the Accessibility screen.

4. Tap Touch Accommodations Keys to display the Touch Accommodations screen.

5. If you tend to keep your tapping finger on the screen too long, tap the Hold Duration switch to On, as shown in Figure 11-10, and then use the Seconds setting to specify how long iOS should allow you to hold the screen before it assumes you're performing a tap-and-hold gesture.

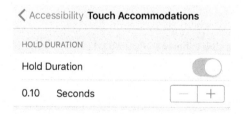

Figure 11-10. *Tap Hold Duration to On to prevent long presses from being interpreted as tap-and-holds*

6. If you tend to bounce your tapping finger on the screen, tap the Ignore Repeat switch to On, and then use the Seconds setting to specify how long iOS should wait before it interprets the gesture as multiple taps rather than a single tap.

7. If you tend to move your tapping finger along the screen, tell iOS to interpret the gesture as a tap rather than a slide by tapping one of the following in the Tap Assistance section:

   - **Use Initial Touch Location.** Tap this setting to use the position where your tapping finger first touches the screen as the tap location.

   - **Use Final Touch Location.** Tap this setting to use the position where your tapping finger stops or leaves the screen as the tap location.

Surmounting Hearing Challenges

If your hearing has deteriorated over the years, or if you have a hearing impairment in one or both ears, detecting device sounds and enjoying music and movies can be a challenge. Fortunately, help is at hand. iOS has a few settings and tools that you can configure to help or work around your hearing issues.

Headphone Sounds Are Unbalanced

Sometimes, hearing troubles in one ear are particularly bad. Adjusting the device volume is problematic in these cases, because turning up the sound enough to hear things in your bad ear can make those sounds too loud in your other ear.

Solution: iOS can help by enabling you to balance the sound in each ear. That is, you can turn up the sound for your bad ear and/or turn down the sound for your good ear.
Here are the steps to follow:

1. On the Home screen, tap Settings to open the Settings app.

2. Tap General to display the General screen.

3. Tap Accessibility to display the Accessibility screen.

4. Under the Hearing section, use the slider shown in Figure 11-11 to adjust the balance between the left and right channels.

Figure 11-11. *To compensate for poor hearing in one ear, use this slider to adjust the audio balance between the left and right channels*

You Can't Hear Alerts

When iOS displays a notification for a text message or incoming email message, it often displays a banner for a few seconds and plays a sound. If you're not near your device to see the banner, and if your hearing is impaired, then you might easily miss the alert.

Solution: On your iPhone (this feature isn't available on other iOS devices), you can tell iOS to flash the camera's LED light a few times, which gives you a visual signal that an alert has occurred.

Follow these steps to set this up:

1. On the Home screen, tap Settings to open the Settings app.

2. Tap General to display the General screen.

3. Tap Accessibility to display the Accessibility screen.

4. In the Hearing section, tap LED Flash for Alerts.

5. Tap the LED Flash for Alerts switch to On, as shown in Figure 11-12.

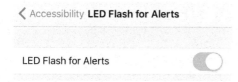

Figure 11-12. *Tap LED Flash for Alerts to On to have iOS flash the camera's LED light when an alert comes in*

6. If you also want iOS to flash the LED even when you have the Ring/Silent switch set to Silent, tap the Flash on Silent switch to On.

■ ■ ■

CHAPTER 12

Troubleshooting Other iOS Problems

So far in this book you have learned not only a number of general problem-solving techniques, but also how to troubleshoot and work around a wide variety of issues. To make it easier to find these problems (or, in many cases, to prevent problems before they happen), these issues have been focused and grouped according to specific topic areas. These have included cellular, Wi-Fi, apps, web browsing, email, phone calls, cameras, photos, device protection, privacy, the battery, and accessibility. That's a wide-ranging list, but there are plenty of iOS troubles that don't it fit into any of these categories.

The purpose of this chapter is to gather together a selection of the most common of these miscellaneous problems, annoyances, and head-scratchers, and to provide solution and workarounds to complete your iOS troubleshooting education.

Troubleshooting Miscellaneous Problems

I'll begin this chapter with a look at a few miscellaneous problems that can make your iOS device easier to use and more efficient.

You Find It Difficult to Reach Items at the Top of the iPhone Screen

The large height of the iPhone 6, 6s, and 7 (not to mention their even bigger Plus versions) means that even people with average-size hands can find it quite a stretch to reach items at or near the top of the screen when they're using the device one-handed.

Solution: Double-tap the Home button, by which I mean you lightly tap the button rather than firmly pressing it. This slides the current screen's contents down about half way, making it much easier to access those items at top, especially when you're using the phone one-handed. To push the screen back up, either double-tap the Home button once again or tap in the blank area above the screen contents (you can also wait about eight seconds and the screen will restore itself automatically).

© Paul McFedries 2017
P. McFedries, *Troubleshooting iOS*, DOI 10.1007/978-1-4842-2445-8_12

Double-Tapping the Home Button Doesn't Do Anything

In the previous section you learned that you can reach items at the top of the big iPhone 6 (and later) screen by double-tapping the Home button. However, you might find that this technique doesn't work for you.

Solution: Here are a few troubleshooting techniques to try:

- Remember that this feature is only available on the iPhone, not the iPad or iPod touch. And, as of this writing, the only iPhone models that support this feature are the 6, 6 Plus, 6s, 6s Plus, 7, and 7 Plus.

- If you see the multitasking screen (that is, the screen that shows all your running or recently run apps), it means you're double-*clicking* the Home button rather than double-*tapping* it. Two light taps are all you need.

- This feature is called Reachability and it's an accessibility setting. If it doesn't work for you, it might mean that the setting has been turned off. To check, follow these steps:

1. On the Home screen, tap Settings to open the Settings app.

2. Tap General to open the General screen.

3. Tap Accessibility to open the Accessibility screen.

4. Tap the Reachability switch to On, as shown in Figure 12-1.

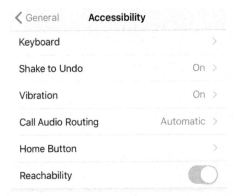

Figure 12-1. *Make sure the Reachability setting is On to enable Home button double-tapping*

Your iOS Device Disturbs You at Inconvenient Times

If you're in a meeting, at a movie, or going to sleep, you don't want your iOS device disturbing the peace with incoming phone calls or alerts. Most people handle this by activating Airplane mode, which turns off all the antennas on the device. That ensures you're distraction free for a while, but it suffers from a major drawback: Without any working antennas, your device can't communicate with the world, so it doesn't download messages or perform any other online activities. That might be what you want, but it's less than optimum if you're expecting something important. Plus, you have to *remember* to activate Airplane mode, something you can't always do when you're busy.

Solution: Configure Do Not Disturb mode, which silences all device distractions – including Notification Center alerts and phone calls – but keeps your device online so that it can continue to receive data. That way, when you're ready to get back to the action, all your new data is already on your device, so you can get back up to speed quickly. To activate Do Not Disturb, open Settings, tap Do Not Disturb, and then tap the Manual switch to On.

You can get the most out of Do Not Disturb by configuring it to suit the way you work. Here are the steps to follow:

1. On the Home screen, tap Settings to open the Settings app.

2. Tap Do Not Disturb to display the Do Not Disturb screen.

3. To set a time to automatically activate and deactivate Do Not Disturb, tap the Scheduled switch to On, as shown in Figure 12-2. You then tap the From/To control; use From to set the start time and use To to set the end time, then tap Back to return to the Do Not Disturb screen.

■ **Note** Rather than scheduling Do Not Disturb mode, you can invoke it at any time by following steps 1 and 2 to display the Do Not Disturb screen, then tapping the Manual switch to On.

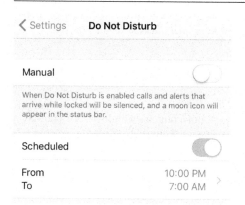

Figure 12-2. *Tap the Scheduled switch to On and then set a start and end time for Do Not Disturb*

4. If you want to allow certain calls even when Do Not Disturb is activated, tap Allow Calls From and then tap who you want to get through: Everyone, No One, Favorites (that is, anyone in the Phone app's Favorites list), or a particular contact group.

5. If you want Do Not Disturb to allow a call through when the same person calls twice within three minutes, leave the Repeated Calls switch in the On position. If you don't want to allow this exception, tap the Repeated Calls switch to Off.

6. If you want Do Not Disturb to handle calls and notifications normally (that is, non-silently) when your device is unlocked, tap the Only While *Device* is Locked option (where *Device* is iPhone, iPad, or iPod).

The Onscreen Keyboard Clicks Are Driving You (and Everyone Near You) Crazy

By default, the iOS onscreen keyboard makes a clicking noise each time you tap a key. Apple must think this aural feedback is useful since the clicks are on by default, but I don't know anyone who doesn't find them annoying and purposeless. Even if you don't mind the incessant clicking, I guarantee that every person within earshot of your device is cursing you silently (or perhaps not so silently).

Solution: Turn off the keyboard clicks by following these steps:

1. On the Home screen, tap Settings to open the Settings app.

2. Tap Sounds to display the Sounds screen.

3. Tap the Keyboard Clicks switch to Off, as shown in Figure 12-3.

Keyboard Clicks

Figure 12-3. To type blissfully noise free, tap the Keyboard Clicks switch to Off

When You Type Two or More Spaces, iOS Always Adds a Period (.) Before the Spaces

This is actually, as the programmers say, a feature, not a bug. It's a built-in shortcut that enables you to end most sentences efficiently with a quick double-tap on the space key.

Solution: If you'd rather be able to enter multiple spaces without the period showing up, you can turn off the shortcut. Here are the steps to follow:

1. On the Home screen, tap Settings to open the Settings app.

2. Tap General to display the General screen.

3. Tap Keyboard to display the Keyboards screen.

4. Tap the "." Shortcut switch to Off, as shown in Figure 12-4.

Figure 12-4. To type two spaces without getting a period (.), tap the "." Shortcut switch to Off

You Can't Type in Another Language

Your iOS device is set up with a default keyboard appropriate to your location, and it also comes with a keyboard of Emoji symbols. If you want to type in another language such as Arabic, Greek, or Russian, there is no direct way to do it using the default keyboard.

Solution: You need to install a new keyboard layout for the language (or languages) you want to use. Here are the steps to follow:

1. On the Home screen, tap Settings to open the Settings app.

2. Tap General to display the General screen.

3. Tap Keyboard to display the Keyboards screen.

4. Tap Keyboards to open the Keyboards screen, which displays a list of installed keyboards.

5. Tap Add New Keyboard to display the Add New Keyboard screen.

6. Tap the keyboard layout you want to use.

To switch from one layout to another, display the onscreen keyboard and then tap and hold the Keyboard button (which is to the right of the 123 or ?123 button). This displays a list of the installed keyboards, as shown in Figure 12-5, and you then tap the layout you want to use.

Figure 12-5. *Tap and hold the Keyboard button to see a list of your installed keyboard layouts*

Your Device Display Is Too Harsh for Night Use

Many of us keep our iOS device at our bedside to use as a clock or alarm. Dimming the display is a must for nighttime use, but for many people the screen colors are still too harsh and they can make it hard to get to sleep.

Solution: You can use the Night Shift feature to shift the screen colors toward the red end of the spectrum. This gives the screen a "warmer" feel overall, which makes it less harsh for night viewing and is more conducive to sleep.

Follow these steps to activate and configure Night Shift:

1. On the Home screen, tap Settings to open the Settings app.

2. Tap Display & Brightness to display the Display & Brightness screen.

3. Tap Night Shift to display the Night Shift screen.

4. To set a time to automatically activate and deactivate Night Shift, tap the Scheduled switch to On, as shown in Figure 12-6. You then tap the From/To control; use From to set the start time and use To to set the end time, then tap Back to return to the Night Shift screen.

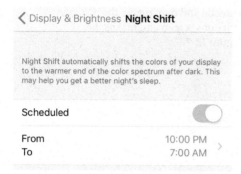

❮ Display & Brightness **Night Shift**

Night Shift automatically shifts the colors of your display
to the warmer end of the color spectrum after dark. This
may help you get a better night's sleep.

Scheduled

From   10:00 PM
To   7:00 AM

Figure 12-6. Tap the Scheduled switch to On and then set a start and end time for Night Shift

---

■ **Note**   Rather than scheduling Night Shift, you can invoke it at any time by following steps 1 to 3 to display the Night Shift screen, then tapping the Manually Enable Until Tomorrow switch to On.

---

5. Use the Color Temperature slider to adjust the screen colors to make them more warm (slide to the right) or less warm (slide to the left).

You Want to Control What Your Children See and Do on an iOS Device

If your children have access to your iOS device, or if they have devices of their own, then you might be a bit worried about some of the content they might be exposed to on the Web, on YouTube, or in iTunes. Similarly, you might not want them installing apps or giving away their current location.

Solution: For all those and similar parental worries, you can sleep better at night by activating the iOS parental controls. These controls restrict the content and activities that kids can see and do. Here's how to set them up:

1. On the Home screen, tap Settings. The Settings app appears.

2. Tap General. The General screen appears.

3. Tap Restrictions. The Restrictions screen appears.

4. Tap Enable Restrictions. iOS displays the Enable Restrictions screen, which you use to specify a four-digit code that you can use to make changes to the parental controls. (Note that this code is not the same as the passcode lock that I discuss earlier in this book; see Chapter 8, "Protecting Your Device.")

5. Tap the four-digit restrictions passcode and then retype the code. iOS returns you to the Restrictions screen and makes the controls available, as shown in Figure 12-7.

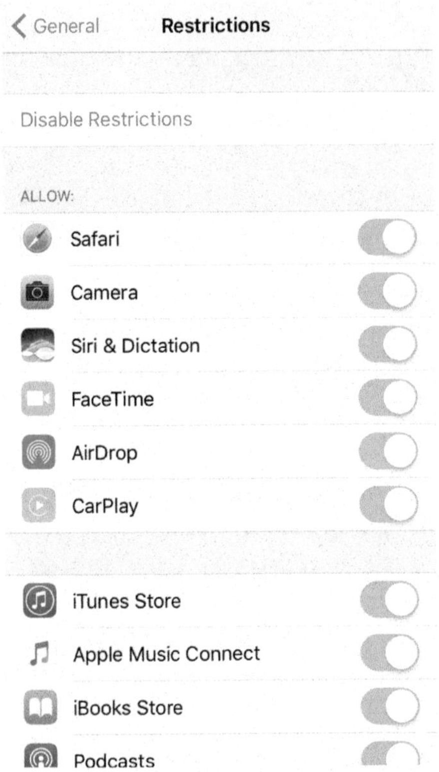

Figure 12-7. *Use the Restrictions screen to configure the parental controls you want to use*

6. In the Allow section, for each app or task, tap the On/Off switch to allow or disallow your child to use the app or task.

7. Under Allowed Content, tap Ratings For and then tap the country with the ratings you want to use.

8. For each of the content controls – Music, Podcasts & News, Movies, TV Shows, Books, Apps, Siri, and Websites – tap the control and then tap the highest rating for the content you want your children to use.

9. If you don't want your children to make changes to certain settings, such as Location Services and Contacts, tap the corresponding setting types in the Privacy section and then tap Don't Allow Changes.

10. If you don't want your children to make changes to the current Mail, Calendar, or Contacts account settings, tap Accounts under Allow Changes, and then tap Don't Allow Changes.

11. If you don't want your children to adjust the maximum volume limit you've set, tap Volume Limit, and then tap Don't Allow Changes.

■ **Tip**   To set the maximum volume on the iOS device, open the Settings app, tap Music, tap Volume Limit, and then use the Max Volume slider to set the limit.

---

12. In the Game Center section, tap the On/Off switches to enable or disable multiplayer games, adding friends, and recording the screen.

Troubleshooting Connection and Syncing Problems

With most syncing running through iCloud these days, many people find they rarely have to connect their iOS device to their computer. However, if you don't have an iCloud account, then connecting to your computer and syncing through iTunes is required, so all the more reason to make sure things are working properly.

iTunes Doesn't See Your Device

When you connect your iOS device to your computer, iTunes should start and you should see the device in the Devices list. If iTunes doesn't start when you connect your device, or if iTunes is already running but the device doesn't appear in the Devices list, it means that iTunes doesn't recognize your device.

Solution: Here are some possible fixes:

- **Trust the computer.** You can't connect to iTunes until you've told iOS that you trust the computer that's running iTunes. On your device, tap Trust.

- **Check the connections.** Make sure the USB connector and the Lightning connector are fully seated.

- **Try a different USB port.** The port you're using might not work, so try another one. If you're using a port on a USB hub, try using one of the computer's built-in USB ports.

- **Try a different cable.** It's possible that the USB cable is defective, so try a different cable if you have one.

- **Restart your device.** Press and hold the Sleep/Wake button for a few seconds until the device shuts down. Press and hold Sleep/Wake again until you see the Apple logo.

- **Restart your computer.** This should reset the computer's USB ports, which might solve the problem.

- **Check your iTunes version.** You need at least iTunes version 12.5.1 to work with iOS 10.

- **Check your operating system version.** On a Mac, your iOS device running iOS 10 requires OS X Mavericks (10.9) or later. On a Windows PC, your iOS device requires Windows 7.

iTunes Won't Sync Your Device

iTunes might see your iOS device, but it might refuse to sync the device.

Solution: It could be a couple of things. First, connect your device, switch to iTunes on your computer, and then click your device in the Devices list. On the Summary tab (see Figure 12-8), make sure the Automatically sync when this *device* is connected check box is selected (where *device* is iPhone, iPad, or iPod).

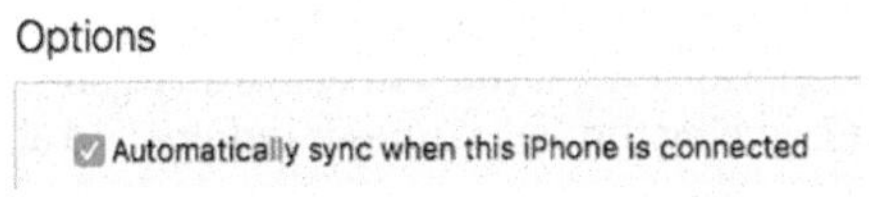

Options

☑ Automatically sync when this iPhone is connected

Figure 12-8. *Select the Automatically sync when this device is connected check box*

If that check box was already selected, then you need to delve a bit deeper to solve the mystery. Follow these steps:

1. Open the iTunes preferences:

    - **Mac.** Click iTunes and then click Preferences.

    - **Windows.** Click Edit and then click Preferences.

2. Click the Devices tab.

3. Deselect the Prevent iPods, iPhones, and iPads from syncing automatically check box.

4. Click OK to put the new setting into effect and enable automatic syncing once again.

Another possibility is that your iOS device is currently locked. That's not usually a problem for iTunes, but it sometimes gets confused by a locked device. The easy remedy is to disconnect the device, unlock it, and then connect it in again.

You Have Trouble Syncing Music or Videos

You may run into a problem syncing your music or videos to your iOS device.

Solution: The most likely culprit here is that your files are in a format that iOS can't read, such as WMA, MPEG-1, or MPEG-2. First, convert the files to a format that iOS does understand using converter software (such as Format Factory; see www.pcfreetime.com/). Then put them back on iTunes and try to sync again. This should solve the problem.

iOS-supported audio formats include AAC, Protected AAC, HE-AAC, MP3, MP3 VBR, Audible (formats 2, 3, and 4; Audible Enhanced Audio; AAX; and AAX+), Apple Lossless, AIFF, and WAV. iOS-supported video formats include H.264, MPEG-4, and Motion JPEG.

An App Opens Each Time You Connect Your Device

Each time you connect your iOS device to your computer, you might see the Photos app (on your Mac) or the AutoPlay dialog box (in Windows). This is certainly convenient if you actually want to send photos to your computer, but you might find that you do that only once in a blue moon. In that case, having to deal with iPhoto or a dialog box every time is frustrating and time consuming.

Solution: You can configure your computer not to pester you about getting photos from your iOS device.

■ **Note**   Configuring your computer not to download photos from your iOS device means that in the future, you'll either need to reverse the setting to get photos or manually import them.

Here's how you set this up on your Mac:

1. Click Spotlight, type image, and then click Image Capture. The Image Capture application opens.

2. In the Devices list, click your iOS device.

3. At the bottom of the Devices pane, click the Connecting this camera opens menu, and then choose No application, as shown in Figure 12-9.

Figure 12-9. *In the Mac's Image Capture program, choose No application to prevent Photos from starting when you connect your iOS device*

4.   Click Image Capture and then click Quit Image Capture.
Image Capture saves the new setting and then shuts down.
The next time you connect your iOS device, Photos ignores it.

Follow these steps to convince Windows not to open the AutoPlay dialog box each
time you connect your iOS device:

1.   Open the Default Programs window:

- **Windows 10.** In the taskbar's Search box, type default and
then click Default Programs.

- **Windows 8.** In the Start screen, type default and then click
Default Programs.

- **Windows 7.** Click Start and then click Default Programs to
open the Default Programs window.

2.   Click Change AutoPlay settings. The AutoPlay dialog box
appears.

3.   In the Devices section, open the list for your iOS device and
choose Take no action, as shown in Figure 12-10.

Figure 12-10. *In the list for your iOS device, choose Take no action to prevent the AutoPlay
dialog box from appearing when you connect your iOS device*

4.   Click Save. Windows saves the new setting. The next time
you connect your iOS device, you won't be bothered by the
AutoPlay dialog box.

Index

© Paul McFedries 2017
P. McFedries, *Troubleshooting iOS*, DOI 10.1007/978-1-4842-2445-8

Get the eBook for only $4.99!

Why limit yourself?

Now you can take the weightless companion with you wherever you go and access your content on your PC, phone, tablet, or reader.

Since you've purchased this print book, we are happy to offer you the eBook for just $4.99.

Convenient and fully searchable, the PDF version enables you to easily find and copy code—or perform examples by quickly toggling between instructions and applications.

To learn more, go to http://www.apress.com/us/shop/companion or contact support@apress.com.

CPSIA information can be obtained
at www.ICGtesting.com
Printed in the USA
LVOW01s1753050117
510800LV00005B/16/P

33164300016701

9 781484 224441